NOVICE
EVENTING
WITH MARK TODD

NOVICE
EVENTING
WITH MARK TODD

with GENEVIEVE MURPHY

Trafalgar Square Publishing

First published in the United States of America in 1996 by Trafalgar Square
Publishing, North Pomfret, Vermont 05053, in association with
David Bateman Limited, Tarndale Grove, Albany Business Park,
North Shore, Auckland, New Zealand

ISBN 1-57076-054-3

Library of Congress Catalog Card Number
95-62233

Photographs by Kit Houghton Photography
Design by Errol McLeary
Typeset by Process Art Studios, Auckland, New Zealand
Printed in Hong Kong by Colorcraft Limited

CONTENTS

INTRODUCTION

From the age of seven, when my grandfather borrowed a pony and taught me to ride, I knew that I would always want to be involved with horses. Children in many parts of the world have probably felt the same way once they discovered the pleasure of being with ponies — feeding and brushing them as well as riding them, in my case for hours on end. I had always liked animals, but there has to be something very special about the ones that you can ride and jump.

Again like many other youngsters, I had my first taste of eventing through a pony club. I belonged to the Cambridge branch in New Zealand and my first important goal was to compete in the pony club championships. But, although twice chosen as reserve for my branch, I never quite made it. Those two near-misses probably had the effect of making me more competitive.

The great thing about eventing is that you can enjoy it at all sorts of levels, whether you are a weekend rider looking for some extra fun and excitement or, like myself, a fairly competitive person who wants to be able to compete at the top level. You do not need a big string of expensive horses or limitless funds at your disposal. Most people begin with just one horse that they look after themselves, which was how I started in senior contests.

To begin with I was more involved in showjumping (then a summer sport in New Zealand) than with eventing, which we did during the winter. There was no overlapping of the seasons so I could compete in both sports with the same horse — a lovely, big Thoroughbred called Top Hunter. Though he reached Grade A in showjumping, he proved to have limitations over coloured poles, but he was an absolute natural as an eventer.

Opposite: *With my wife Carolyn at Le Lion d'Angers, one of the well-established events in France.*

Above: *A picturesque setting at Puhinui, New Zealand's newest venue for eventing.*

Top Hunter did five one-day events and one three-day during his first season in eventing. On that rather insubstantial record, we were chosen for the 1978 World Championships, which were held at Lexington in Kentucky.

My stay in America, where I was based for ten months before the championships, ended with my horse breaking down on the cross-country day so we did not complete the course. We had been tenth after the dressage and I felt that Top Hunter would have been capable of jumping clear across country but for his injury; had he done so we could have won the world title. I was probably hooked on eventing already, but it was the realisation that I could be competitive at a top level that gave me a sharper sense of direction. The die was cast and I am now a three-day event rider who makes occasional dabbles into show-jumping, which I still enjoy.

Eventing has since grown enormously and it now has well-established contests in most parts of the world. But its principal home is in Britain, where I have been based since 1984. Like many others I moved here because of the crowded calendar of events which caters for horses at all levels. Countries that are regularly represented at British one-day events include Australia, Sweden, the United States, Canada, the Netherlands, Germany, Japan, Korea and, of course, New Zealand.

This book deals only with one-day eventing, which is where every horse and rider begins wherever they happen to live. These contests cater for a wide variety of ambitions but, whether your aims are modest or far-reaching, you will want to compete to the best of your ability. I hope that this book will help you to get off to a good start.

Mark Todd

Chapter 1

THE RIGHT HORSE

The crucial thing to remember when you set out in search of the right horse is to find one that suits your own needs. That may sound like stating the obvious, but it happens to be a point that too many people overlook. You do not necessarily want a world-beating three-day eventer when you are starting out in the sport.

I was lucky enough to have a very good pony called Little Man when I rode in my first pony club one-day event in New Zealand at the age of 14. He was three-quarter Arab and as generous as they come, but I have since encountered horses with a predominance of Arab blood that seemed rather less enthusiastic about jumping cross-country fences and I now have some reservations about the breed.

You can ride virtually any horse in a novice event as long as it enjoys jumping. I have become

Opposite: Salvador Dali displays his excellent jumping technique; a perfect example of a horse that tucks his knees under his chin.

a Thoroughbred fan, but the novice rider would probably do better with a horse that has at least a quarter — and possibly a half — non-Thoroughbred blood. One that has done some hunting or show-jumping would be ideal for a novice. Difficulties can arise when you have an inexperienced rider trying to teach a novice horse. If the horse hasn't learnt to jump, you would need to be naturally very talented, or have a lot of expert help, to avoid running into problems.

I love buying horses; it is almost an addiction. A new horse is like a new toy and I can't wait to play with it. Obviously, I am always looking for a horse that might make a good three-day eventer and, because producing and selling are part of my business, I want one that might suit a variety of different people. Having said that, my ideal horse would not necessarily suit every rider.

If you are buying a horse that you want to event yourself, you have a number of specific things to consider, such as your own height,

Charisma's head expresses interest and intelligence. Note the calm eye, with width between the eyes, the large nostril and, above all else, the wonderful outlook.

Just an Ace has a worried looking eye, but maybe I'm seeing that because I know his personality. He nevertheless has a pleasing outlook.

weight, strength, competence and experience. It goes without saying that a slightly built girl of 1.57 m (5 ft 2 in) would not want a Thoroughbred of 17 hands. Nor would a person who had just taken up riding at the age of 45 and was a bit nervous; in that case, something steady would be much more appropriate.

If you are worried about jumping, you would need a horse that will impart some of its own confidence to you. If you are not particularly strong, you need to avoid a horse like Ian Stark's former mount, Murphy Himself, who pulled like a train. Above all else, you want to be comfortable on the horse and feel that you can control him.

Head

My own routine when I go to look at a horse begins when I see its head looking over the stable door. I like the horse to have large, intelligent eyes with plenty of width between them, nice big ears and a large nostril. You would not need to bother so much about the size of the nostril if the horse were only competing in one-day events. It becomes more important in three-day events, which test speed and stamina as well as cross-country jumping. The nostril is used for the intake of air; if it is small, it will restrict the amount of air that can be taken into the lungs.

I like the horse's head to be generous and preferably good-looking, but not pretty. If the head were ugly, the horse would have to be a star in other aspects before I'd consider buying it. Having said that, you could easily by-pass the perfect mount for a novice rider simply by having too much of an obsession with appearances.

People tend to go for the horse that looks the perfect part rather than one that moves in a superb way. It is easy to end up with a very good-looking, flashy mover, who might get good

Salvador Dali, who is Carolyn's horse, has a know-it-all head and a very calm outlook.

Killian's head is on the plain side, but thoroughly genuine and honest.

marks in the dressage but is unlikely to complete the cross-country. The steadier, more careful, horse might look more ordinary, but he is the one that will probably jump a double clear round and send you home feeling happy.

Overall picture

You are never going to find the perfect horse, so you have to be prepared to weigh up the pros and cons. On the minus side would be any aspect of the overall picture which suggested that it didn't fit together. For instance, the neck might be too long for the body (or vice versa), and the front or back-end might look as though it belonged on another body. The horse might have a big body stuck on short little legs. I am more concerned with the overall harmony than in the other details you might find in a perfect horse, such as a nice depth of girth and sloping shoulders.

I prefer the horse to be slightly higher at the

wither, or at least to have withers that are level with the hindquarters. It is not easy to know if that will be the case with a very young horse that might not have grown to its full height, but there should not be much change once it has reached four or five years of age.

It is more difficult to balance a horse that is built on a downhill line, but I've had successful ones which answered that description. Bahlua is one such example; he helped me to finish fifth at the 1990 World Equestrian Games where we were part of the winning team. He was later sold to Dutch rider Eddy Stibbe, who rode him for third place at the 1993 European Championships.

Legs and feet

The conformation defects that worry me the most are the ones that can affect the horse's soundness. Those that are badly back at the knee

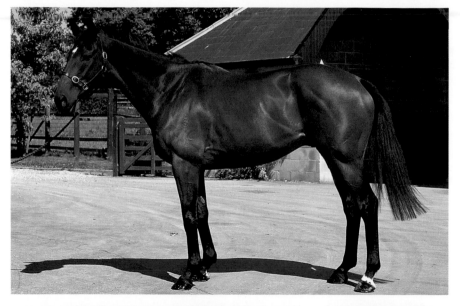

Regal Scot is a New Zealand Thoroughbred with a large nostril and a lovely depth of girth which, theoretically, provides more lung space. He had been racing before I bought him and is therefore much better muscled than most of our other young horses.

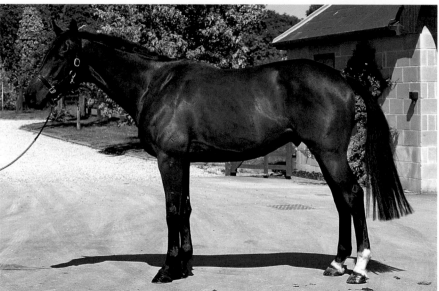

Word for Word, another New Zealand Thoroughbred, has good limbs and bone and he is very strong across the loins. Although his shoulder is straighter than most of our other horses, he is a stunning mover with three excellent paces. Having come over from New Zealand, he had grown a winter coat during the English summer and had to be clipped.

Starman is slightly back at the knee, as can be seen when looking at his off foreleg. We nevertheless bought this English Thoroughbred because he had so many other things in his favour.

Charisma looks the ideal type for eventing. He has a deep girth, wonderful limbs and the overall picture is balanced and pleasing.

Admirable is the lighter type of English Thoroughbred, with a lovely head. He is tall and lean and was still quite weak when the photograph was taken at the beginning of his sixth year. He is a little bit long in the neck and body, but the overall picture is still pleasing.

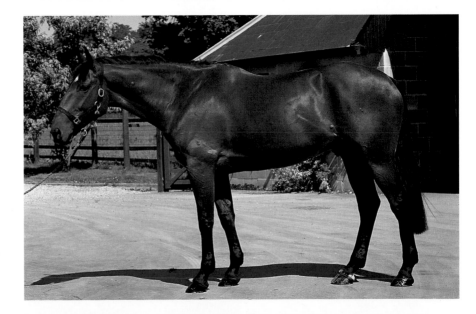

Wise Guy is a typical example of a quality Irish horse. He is three-quarters Thoroughbred, whereas Salvador Dali (also from Ireland) is seven-eighths.

are more likely to have leg trouble because of the extra strain on their tendons. Horses with short and upright pasterns usually have a very jerky action, which is uncomfortable for the rider and another possible cause of injury because of the constant jarring. When you look at the horse head-on, his front legs should be straight. If they come in or go out at the knee, there will be more strain on the joints which can also lead to leg trouble.

I don't like the horse to have a curb on his hock or a splint, but I have bought some that had one or other of these because the pros outweighed the cons to an extent that made it seem worth taking a gamble. I also dislike it when the horse stands with his hindlegs way out behind him. That usually means that he will be very strung out and hard to collect, but I would not necessarily reject him on that alone.

Feet are obviously important since, like everybody else, I want the horse I buy to stay sound. For that reason, I would avoid narrow feet with contracted heels, and, probably, flat feet as well. I do, however, have to be more fussy in this respect than the rider who is just looking to have some fun in one-day events. Any horse that I buy will be aimed at three-day events, which are much more demanding on feet and limbs.

Temperament

Assessing the horse's character is never easy when you see it for the first time. You have to take its surroundings into account; no horse can be expected to have a wonderful outlook on life if it happens to be living in a dive of a place. I have found that horses change their outlook and personality as their education progresses. Nevertheless, I am constantly looking for all those hints and signs that tell me something about the horse's character.

When the horse is led out of its stable, I watch to see how it goes about its work. Is it shy and spooky? Or does it walk with an air of confidence? I watch it being tacked up, not with any wish to condemn the horse but because I am trying to build up a picture of its character and temperament. These will also be considered when he is walked and trotted in hand and, later, when he is ridden and jumped under saddle.

I like the horse to look interested in his surroundings, but to do everything in a calm fashion. If he were to lay back his ears and show signs of not wanting to work, or if he doesn't want to leave the stable yard, he will probably have a difficult temperament and would be best avoided. If he were jumpy and excitable, I would have to decide whether he was displaying youthful high spirits or was a bit of a nut-case. You need to take in as much as you can about the horse in order to be able to assess its temperament.

Action in hand

I find the trot more revealing than the walk when the horse is being led in hand. I want to make sure that the animal is sound and that it trots with level steps, both of which are essential. If it trots like a pneumatic drill, with choppy little strides, I probably wouldn't look any further. Such action would involve too much wear and tear on its feet and legs, as well as causing the rider serious discomfort.

I also like to see how straight the horse moves when it trots towards me. Do its legs go in all directions or do they follow a straight line? I don't mind if the horse swings a leg or dishes a little bit, but I wouldn't want one that twisted a leg quite badly or that flung its legs all over the place.

Viewed from the rear, some horses trot very wide behind. This is not a serious problem, except that dressage judges tend to get uptight about it. If the hindlegs are very close, or if they have a tendency to cross over, the horse is more liable to knock itself and cause an injury. I wouldn't condemn it solely for that reason, but it's something that has to be taken into consideration.

Paces and jumping

I would then want to see the horse being ridden so that I could look at its three basic paces. Ideally, the horse should swing through its body and step well forward in walk rather than taking choppy little strides. The trot should show a good length of stride and an even rhythm. The canter should be as balanced as possible, depending on the horse's level of training. If he finds it easy to keep in canter then you know he has a natural balance. If he struggles a little and breaks into trot when going round a corner, the balance does not come as naturally and will have to be taught.

Next I would want to see the horse being jumped, assuming that he has reached this stage in his education. This can be a deceptive exercise; some horses are so badly ridden that you cannot see their natural talent, while others are ridden so well that you get a false impression of their ability. I will be looking at the horse's attitude to jumping, whether he's a bit spooky or goes

straight to the fence in a confident manner.

I also want to look at his technique. I like to see a good lift of the forearm and bend of the knee in front, with the horse rounding its back and neck so as to make a good shape over the fence. If he uses his back well, he should let go with the back legs and float them out behind. But not all horses do that; some tuck their hind legs up, which is quite acceptable as long as they get them out of the way.

Above all else I want to see whether the horse is careful, which is even more important than technique. Some have a natural desire to avoid hitting fences, while others do not seem to care whether they clobber them or not.

Riding the horse

When I first get on a horse, I like to feel that I am sitting in the middle of its body, with a nice length of rein. Sometimes you find that the neck seems too short, or you feel as though you are perched on its back end. Some horses turn out to be very narrow; others are unexpectedly wide. The latter would be unsuitable for a rider with short legs, because it would be difficult to sit comfortably and to apply the aids correctly.

Having watched somebody else ride the horse, I will know whether it is excitable or calm, well-trained or very green, so I have some idea of what to expect. When I start moving forward, I like to let the horse walk on a loose rein so that he can get used to me while I am assessing his walk. After that I would take up contact and go into trot, without asking for much in the way of outline or impulsion. I want to know if the horse has a choppy stride or, maybe, a very long stride; and whether it is in balance and responsive to the rider.

I am not looking for a big, flashy trot, but for a nice, even rhythm. If the rhythm comes naturally, training is always much easier. I also like to ask the horse to lengthen within the trot to see if he does this naturally, which would be another plus point.

When cantering, I want to feel that the horse is in balance, though I wouldn't expect too much if he were very young, green or inexperienced. I will be aware of whether I have to kick to keep him in canter and if I need to hang onto his head to keep him balanced. Both of these would indicate that the horse lacks natural balance and that he will have to learn it through schooling. If I can feel a jar coming up through his shoulder, I would know that he is susceptible to injury because his feet hit the ground so hard.

I would always advise a novice rider to avoid a horse with a great long canter stride. He will be difficult to control and balance in canter, and it will be hard to see a stride when riding him to a fence. On the other hand, I would not like a short, choppy canter; this would put extra strain on the horse's legs and sitting to it could be very difficult.

When I start jumping, I like to let the horse trot into a little fence so that I can get an idea of its attitude. I do as little as possible in the way of giving it help, because I want to see the horse's own natural reaction as he comes to the fence and jumps it. I would not have a loose rein, but the contact would be fairly light. Instead of trying to place the horse, I would be letting him make the decisions himself. Much depends on how horses have been ridden; some tend to spook and back off, while others have acquired the bad habit of rushing at fences.

I like to play around on the horse, trotting and cantering over small obstacles. I want him to give

me the feeling that he is looking at each fence and paying attention to it. You obviously have to make allowances if he hasn't done much jumping before, in which case it will be more difficult to assess his jumping ability. When he comes to the fence, I like the horse to make an effort to clear it with a proper jump rather than stepping over it.

If possible I have my wife, Carolyn, there to tell me whether the horse is picking up its knees or letting its legs dangle. I might have got the wrong impression while I was watching it jump. A clever rider, who was producing the horse for sale, could do little, inconspicuous things that help to disguise any shortcomings in its technique.

Some horses can give you an amazing feeling over a fence, but then you find that their front legs were dangling. Others don't give much of a feeling, but it turns out that they were being very neat and tidy. I would definitely avoid any horse that repeatedly hit the fences or felt unsafe.

The novice rider should be looking for a horse that jumps in a safe way. Anything really spooky should be regarded with great caution; the horse would probably need a strong leg aid. If the rider lacks experience and is not sufficiently positive, this would definitely be the wrong sort of horse. The novice rider does not need a spectacular jumper so much as one that jumps in a neat, confident fashion, without attempting to stop or run out. It will be difficult to sort out problems if you are still learning yourself. You should look for a horse that basically wants to please its rider and will help to give you confidence.

Stable vices

I would be prepared to put up with some stable vices, such as weaving, crib-biting, wind-sucking or box-walking (box-stall walking), if the horse was perfect in every other way. I have had horses with one or other of these vices and it didn't affect their performance. However, they are annoying habits which can easily be copied by others, so you have to accept that the horse would probably be unwelcome in most stable yards.

Box-walking, whereby the horse keeps moving round and round his stable, is usually restricted to highly strung Thoroughbred types, but the other stable vices are more widespread. Wind-sucking, by which the horse sucks in air and swallows it, would worry me most. In extreme cases, it can be detrimental to his health.

Most people would wish to avoid any horse that bites or kicks. It could signify that he has a malicious streak in him, though sometimes it stems from bad handling and can be overcome. You would nevertheless have to regard such a horse as potentially dangerous, especially if there are young children around.

Below: *A good example of a balanced horse cantering over poles.*

Avoiding the pitfalls

The second horse I bought when I was getting started in eventing was a mistake, but not a complete disaster. I bought him on somebody else's recommendation, even though I didn't particularly like his jumping technique when I went to try him. Looking back I realise that I should have trusted my own judgement a bit more. I also made the mistake of thinking that I could improve his technique, whereas that is something that you can rarely do much about.

If the horse has been allowed to develop bad habits over a number of years, it will be difficult to change its ways and I wouldn't even attempt it. Through mistakes in the past I have now learnt my lesson in thinking that I can transform horses with poor technique or ingrained bad habits.

Vetting

The horse needs to be sound, so it will have to be seen by a vet before you part with your money.

Wilton Fair may not look the perfect picture, but he could do the job. It was the biggest surprise of my life to win Burghley with him.

Having said that, you need to be aware that some vets seem to find it difficult to pass any horse with a clean bill of health, probably because they are worried about litigation. I have known a horse to be failed because it needed shoeing! You should therefore try to find a vet with a knowledge of the sport, who is known to be realistic in his or her assessments. Failing that, you should try to get an experienced person's interpretation of the veterinary report.

The ideal type

Of all the horses I have ever ridden, Charisma came closest to being the perfect type of event horse, except, perhaps, for his size. He was only 15.3 hands and I am 1.9 m (6 ft 2½ in); when I first went to try him he looked like a fat, slightly overgrown pony and I wondered how anyone could have suggested that he might make a suitable mount for me. Little did I realise that we would win two individual Olympic gold medals together!

Although small, Charisma had the ideal conformation for an event horse. He also had a natural aptitude for dressage and cross-country, but he could be a little careless when show-jumping and tended to have the odd rail down. When he was 21 I gave a dressage display on him in New Zealand and, even at that age, his dressage was better than any of the horses that were stabled at my yard in England.

Charisma was bred in New Zealand, which has been the birthplace of many good event horses. I may be prejudiced, but I think that New Zealand horses are a little more athletic, wiry and tough (both physically and mentally) than those from any other part of the world. But I would happily buy a horse from anywhere else if it were an athletic type and matched my own criteria of acceptability. England, Ireland, France and the United States are among the countries that produce some excellent horses.

Some Irish horses can be on the heavy side if they have a lot of draught blood, so I would prefer one that was ⅞ Thoroughbred. Having said that, I won the Burghley Horse Trials on a three-quarter bred Irish horse called Wilton Fair. He was 17 hands and a bit on the plain side, but he could do the job and that, after all, is what matters most.

Summary

General points
- Find a horse to suit your own needs
- Do not be obsessed with appearances
- Do not expect perfection
- Be prepared to weigh up the pros and cons

Paces
- At walk: the horse should swing through its body and step well forward
- At trot: should take level steps, with a good length of stride and an even rhythm
- At canter: should be as balanced as possible, depending on age and level of training
- A horse with short, choppy strides will be prone to injury

Jumping
- Horse should approach the fence in a confident manner
- Should show a good lift of forearm and bend of knee
- Should round its back over the fence
- Should be careful

Avoiding pitfalls
- Beware of conformation defects that can make a horse prone to injury: badly back at the knee; short and upright pasterns; narrow feet with contracted heels
- Avoid a horse with short, choppy strides (also prone to injury)
- Do not buy a horse with a difficult temperament
- Remember that you can rarely improve on jumping technique
- Avoid a horse with ingrained bad habits

Best buy for novice rider
- Horse with some non-Thoroughbred blood
- One that jumps in a safe way
- Horse that does not attempt to stop or run out
- One that wants to please its rider
- Horse that is an uncomplicated ride

My ideal type
- Charisma — preferably one hand higher!

Chapter 2

HORSE MANAGEMENT

Whether the horse is kept in a stable or outside in a field will depend on the climate and individual circumstances. If you have only one horse, it is probably easier to keep it in a paddock. Then it doesn't matter if you can't ride for a day or so; if it is out in the field the horse can exercise itself. There is no need for him to be stabled in order to compete in one-day events. At home in New Zealand, where we have milder winters than in Europe and the United States, I have three-day evented horses straight from the field.

If you have a lot of horses in work, as I normally do, it is more practical to keep them stabled, especially when the weather is terribly wet. Our young horses and any that are highly strung are the only ones that spend most of their time out in the fields.

Ideally I would like all of them to be out there for part of the day, but we don't always achieve this in our busy yard. Being outside is a much healthier environment, as long as the horse doesn't get too fat. If it does put on too much weight, it will have to spend part of the day in the stable or in a fairly bare paddock to stop it from endless gorging.

Feeding

Unless they need to slim down a bit, the stabled horses have as much good quality hay as they want, but we obviously avoid wasting it. We don't normally soak the hay; this is only done if any of the horses has a problem with its breathing because of a dust allergy.

Unless they need building up, those living outside would probably have two feeds a day other than grass when they are in work. Those kept inside have three feeds, plus one extra feed at night during the latter stages of preparation for a three-day event. This routine only changes on their one rest-day a week, when we turn them out in the field unless it's terribly wet and muddy. We usually omit the lunch-time feed on their day off and we would probably cut down on the night feed as well.

The availability of excellent mixed feeds has proved a boon to people who keep horses, and it has done a lot to reduce the guesswork involved for novice riders. The quality was a bit dubious when mixes first came on the market, but nowadays you can rely on them being good. Horses in my yard used to be given much more grain, such as oats and barley, than they have now.

Here in Britain, all our novices compete on Badminton Horse Feeds mix (sweet feed) or cubes (pellets), with alfalfa usually added at breakfast and supper. There are plenty of choices on the market, so you can always find a mix suitable for your horse's temperament and the work it is doing. You can have high or low energy mixes, others for horses that tend to put on too much weight or who need building up. Mixed feeds have the great advantage of eliminating the chore of buying all the ingredients separately.

It is obviously important to consider each horse's individual needs. One may require something extra because he's a bit thin or lacks energy, and his feeds will be adjusted accordingly. In our yard we would probably give boiled barley and soaked sugar-beet to the thin horse, while some oats should liven up the one that needs more energy. You can, of course, change to a mix that suits your horse's needs. We used to feed bran mashes once a week, which was the traditional thing to do, but it now seems less fashionable. A nutritionist once told me that it was probably a total waste of time and could even upset the horse's stomach, so we no longer bother with them.

The following examples are a rough guide to our feeding regime, which most of our horses settle into quite quickly. You can also obtain a useful guide-line by finding out how the horse was fed by its former owner. At the same time you need to be constantly aware of how the horse feels and looks, so that you know whether an adjustment to his diet would be beneficial.

We keep the quantities for each horse written on a blackboard, which means that anyone in the yard can take charge of the feeding. The following amounts were given to four of our horses in mid-February. Jack was then a novice in light work and Henry (also a novice) was preparing to compete in one-day events the following month. Bertie was getting ready for Badminton, which was then 11 weeks away. Bubble was a newly broken horse who was a bit too full of himself, so his diet consisted mainly of bulk food with just a handful of mix twice a day. The amounts are given in scoops.

	Breakfast	Lunch	Supper
JACK			
	1 mix	hay (ad lib)	1 mix
	1 alfalfa		1½ alfalfa
			soaked
			sugar-beet
HENRY			
	1 mix	1 mix	1 mix
	1 alfalfa		1 micronised
			barley
			1 alfalfa
			boiled barley
BERTIE			
	1 mix	1 mix	1 mix
	1 alfalfa		1 micronised
	½ maize		barley
			1 alfalfa
			½ maize
			boiled barley
BUBBLE			
	handful mix	hay (ad lib)	handful mix
	½ bran		½ bran
	1 alfalfa		1 alfalfa
	soaked sugar-beet		

Weights per scoop: micronised barley 1.25 kg (2 lb 12 oz); coarse mix 1 kg (2 lb 4 oz); maize 680g (1 lb 8 oz); 1 alfalfa is equal to a double handful of alfalfa.

There were changes on the blackboard by the end of April, notably against Bertie's name. He is a very lean horse and we had been feeding him with the idea of putting some weight on him

	AM	LUNCH	PM
TOMMY	1A 1M	1M	1A 1M 1B BB
BLOB	1A 1CM	1N	1A 1CM BB
ROBBY	1A 1M ½N	1M	1A 1M 1N 1A
BLUE	1A 1M	1N	1A 1M 1N BB
LADDIE	1A 1M	1M	1A 1M 1B BB
HENRY	1HF 1O ½B	1O	1HF 1O 1S 1B BB
FRED	1HF 1O ½B	—	1HF 1O ½S ½B BB
YOGI	1A 1M	1N	1A 1M 1B BB
JOSH	1A 1M	1M	1A 1M BB
DALI	1A 1M	1M	1A 1M 1B BB
SCOTTIE	1A 1CM		1A 1CM 1B BD
BERTIE	1HF 1O ½B	—	1HF 1O ½S ½B BB
ACE	1A ½CM	—	½A ½CM ½B BB
CHESS	1A 1CM	1CM	1A 2CM 1B BB
KAYEM	1A 1CM	1CM	1A 2CM 1B BB
TENTU	½A ½M	1M	1A 1M 1BB
COPPER	1A 1M SB	1M	1BBSB

The quantities for each horse are written on a blackboard.

Preparing the feed.

and, as a result, his temperament boiled over. He was like a lunatic when I rode him in a pre-Badminton dressage competition and it took many hours of work (cantering, jumping, flat work and lungeing) to get him into the right state of mind for his dressage test at a one-day event the following day.

The problem was made worse by weeks of rain which meant that the horses weren't able to have a spell in the field during the day; they would have ploughed it up and ruined it for later in the year. Being outside always helps them to expend a certain amount of energy and become more relaxed.

Bertie had been on a high energy mix, so we switched him to one that was less stimulating. We also cut out the two half-scoops of maize, which is good for putting on weight but can be quite heating. The maize was replaced by a scoop of low energy cubes with his supper.

There was scarcely any change in the diet for Jack or Henry, and Bubble had been sold, so his name no longer figured on the blackboard.

Additives

Our horses have salt, which can be provided by having a salt-lick in the stable; seaweed, which is full of natural vitamins; and garlic powder, which is good for the lungs and general health.

They also have vitamin supplements, though I am not sure that they are absolutely necessary. If they are fed on a prepared mix, the right vitamins should already be included in their diet. Horses that live outside should be getting all they need in the way of nutrients, especially during the spring and summer when the grass is normally at its best. A commercially prepared supplement that includes calcium can be helpful for the horse's muscle and bone.

I would regard salt or a salt-lick as essential, plus vitamin supplements if these were not already included in the horse's feed. The other additives would not be necessary for a horse competing in novice one-day events.

Dealing with problems

Occasionally you get a fussy eater and you have to experiment a bit, leaving out an ingredient and seeing whether the horse eats what remains, so that you discover his likes and dislikes. Sometimes a horse barely touches his breakfast until he has been worked, but then comes back and eats it all. Some clean up their night feed straight away; others munch their way through it during the night.

We would never put a new feed on top of left-overs; the remains of the previous meal have to be removed first and the feed bowl should be scrubbed clean. Assuming that the horse seemed fit and well, I would cut back on its rations if it was consistently leaving some of its food. It's a waste of money when you have to throw food away and the horse probably doesn't need it anyway.

On the other hand, if you have a horse with a good appetite that suddenly goes off its food, you would have a fairly good indication that something is wrong. Maybe his teeth need attention, or perhaps he has picked up a virus. If the horse looks miserable and lethargic, even though he has a healthy appetite, I might also suspect a viral infection. If in any doubt about the horse's well-being, I would always have him blood-tested to find the cause of the problem.

Feeding at events

When I am competing, the horses' meals have to be fitted in around the times that they do their three phases of the competition. They would still have a lunch feed, but it might be earlier or later than usual. Ideally, I would like the horse to have a minimum of two hours between his lunch and going across country. If he were doing his dressage in the morning and his cross-country late in the afternoon, he would also have a small hay-net to munch between phases. The horse doesn't need to be starved to compete in a one-day event; on the other hand, you wouldn't want him to be finishing off a huge hay-net shortly before going across country. It is really all a matter of common sense.

Stable routine

Whether you have one or twenty horses, you need to have a routine. This can be fairly flexible for the spare-time rider who has work to do at school, in an office or wherever, but the horse

Paper bedding.

should be fed at the same times each day. Stabled horses, in particular, come to anticipate their meal-times and they get understandably fractious if they are kept waiting.

It helps to work out a timetable that includes mucking out, feeding and refilling water buckets (our horses have fresh water available at all times), schooling and exercising, grooming, tack cleaning and bedding down for the night. There are several types of bedding: straw, shavings, shredded paper and hemp. We use Aubiose hemp bedding because it is absorbent, dust-free and easy to dispose of as it decomposes rapidly. Avoid bedding that is dusty or mouldy.

When you first see the horse in the morning, you should acquire the habit of running your hands down its legs and giving it a quick look over. Unless you train yourself to be observant, it

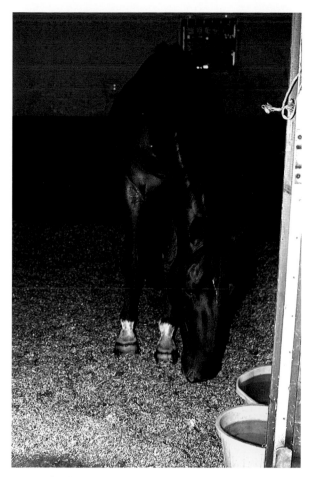

Hemp bedding.

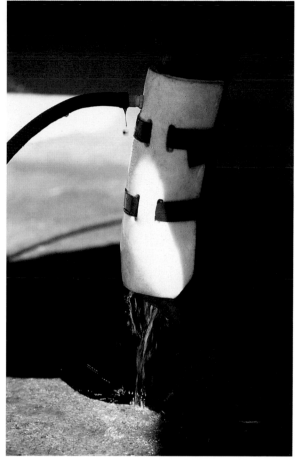

The hose boot is used when a horse has filling or bruising on a leg.

is easy to overlook the early signs, such as heat or swelling in a leg, that warn of a possible problem. Treatment at this stage can prevent it from becoming serious. I can remember how worried we were at finding a lump on Charisma's hind leg ten days before he was due to fly to Los Angeles for the 1984 Olympic Games. We stood him in a whirlpool boot (which is filled with water and has air pumped into it) as often as possible. To my great relief, the lump, which was probably caused by a kick, soon disappeared.

If the horse has heat or swelling from a knock, he should have only light exercise and his ration of energy-giving food should be reduced. On the other hand, exercise would be detrimental if there were heat or swelling in a tendon. Veterinary advice should be sought immediately in either case.

Clipping

Most of our horses are fully clipped during the winter. It makes it easier to keep them clean and it stops them from sweating up when they are working. At that time of year, most of them are preparing for the spring events. They are also stabled, so there is no problem in giving them a full clip as long as they are then rugged up and kept warm.

Sometimes the younger horses just have a trace-clip, which is better for those that are living outside for most of the time. If the horse is fairly hairy and breaks into a sweat after trotting for five minutes, then it obviously makes sense to have him clipped either fully or partially.

Above: *Hosing down after exercise.*

Below: *Using the sweat scraper.*

Removing sweat

It is always necessary to remove sweat from the horse whether it is living in or out. Our horses are washed off with a hose after working unless it is very cold, in which case they are washed over with warm water. They are then kept warm with a Thermatex rug or sweat sheet until they are completely dry and can be given a good brush. You can let the sweat dry without hosing, but it must always be brushed off, with extra care given to the saddle and bridle areas, otherwise sores can occur.

Care after the cross-country

At most events you would expect to take ten minutes or so walking back from the end of the cross-country course to the horse-box/trailer

Above: *This cooler helps the horse to cool off after the cross-country.*

park. This gives the horse time to recover at least partially from his exertion. On a freezing cold day, a rug would be put over his loins and quarters immediately, then the tack and boots removed. If the horse was still blowing, he would be walked in hand until his breathing had returned to normal. He is then washed down. In cold weather, we would only wash his legs and neck. The saddle patch would only be sponged; we would not want to get any water over his back for fear of him getting a chill. On a warm day, the horse would be washed all over to remove sweat and dirt. He is then walked round in a Thermatex rug or a sweat sheet until he has dried off.

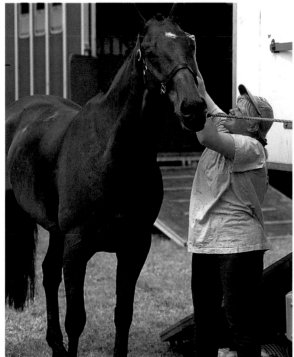

Left: *Sponging the horse's head after the cross-country.*

Above: *Checking the horse's legs for nicks and cuts.*   Below: *Removing the studs.*

While washing the horse we will have checked to see whether he has any nicks or cuts. These would need to be cleaned thoroughly and treated straight away, with wound powder, antiseptic ointment or with an animalintex poultice applied under a bandage, to avoid the risk of infection. If he had a cut which required stitches, we would obviously need to call the vet.

Unless the cross-country is before the show-jumping (as it often is in the United States), the routine I have described precedes the journey home. The horse is watered and his studs are removed before he is loaded into the lorry or van; he is then given a hay-net to eat. He will have his night feed when he is back home in his own stable. I am a great believer in homeopathic remedies, particularly arnica which helps to relieve bruising. So, if the horse has had a knock, arnica tablets would be added to his feed.

Rolling up bandages.

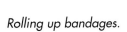

Summary

Feeding
- Consider each horse's individual needs
- Be aware of how the horse looks and feels
- Feed hay ad lib, unless the horse is overweight
- If in doubt about his well-being, have the horse blood-tested

Routine
- Meals should be given at regular times
- Check horse over each morning and run a hand down its legs
- If there is heat or swelling, consult the vet immediately
- Remove sweat after horse has been exercised
- If horse is stabled, turn him out in a field when possible

After the cross-country
- If weather is cold, put on rug immediately
- Remove tack and boots
- If horse is still blowing, walk him until his breathing is normal
- Wash down (only legs, neck and saddle patch in cold weather)
- If horse has any nicks or cuts, treat immediately
- Walk horse round in cooler or sweat sheet until dry
- Give horse water and remove studs before loading him into the lorry or van

Chapter 3

TRAINING ON THE FLAT

Like most people when they start eventing, I used to put up with the dressage so that I could get on with the exciting part of riding across country. But attitudes change; when you've been in the sport for a while you realise that you have to work at the dressage if you want to be successful. You also begin to appreciate the benefits of having a horse that is supple and obedient through working on the flat. Nowadays it is second nature to me to try and improve any horse that I am riding, because I enjoy it so much more when I'm on one that goes correctly.

You do not need a proper arena in order to school a horse, though it's obviously nice to have one. When I started eventing, I used part of a flat field and that was perfectly adequate. And you don't need to be there for hours on end; 20 minutes is ample for a young horse and it would probably be plenty for a novice rider as well.

Opposite: Leg yielding to the left, but with the horse resisting and tilting his head to the left.

The horse obviously needs a certain level of fitness before he can do as much work as that. If he has had several months off, he will need at least two weeks of slow hacking or lungeing before he can start short training sessions on the flat. These could build up to 20 minutes, three or four times a week, with possibly one or two extra during the lead-up to the first event.

You need to have some idea of what you intend to do when you get into the school or field; trotting round and round in endless circles will get you nowhere. During each session you need to think about improving rhythm, contact, outline and transitions. You should also plan to work on one or two specific things that are included in this chapter, so that each lesson is a form of progression for you and the horse.

It would also help to have a rough plan as to what you aim to achieve each month, so that you have a goal on which to focus. Whether or not the goal is reached within that time will obviously depend on the ability of the rider as well as the aptitude of the horse. Problems can arise all too easily, especially if a novice rider is attempting to train an inexperienced horse. If this is the case, you would certainly need some help from a capable trainer, otherwise confusions are bound to crop up when you and the horse are learning together.

We all need help from time to time, no matter what level we have reached. During my pony club days in New Zealand, I was lucky enough to have excellent instructors who drummed into me the correct basics, such as position and how to apply the aids. I may not have appreciated every moment of it at the time, but I am certainly grateful now.

Rider's position

The rider's back should be straight, with head up and looking forward between the horse's ears. The upper body should be almost vertical, with hips slightly forward and the shoulders back and relaxed. Tension in the shoulders will affect the whole arm, so that you end up having a tense contact with the horse. Elbows should hang loosely, slightly in front of the rider's side. If they are behind the body, it means that the reins were too long. A straight line from the elbows, through the arms and reins to the horse's mouth, shows that the hands are in the right place.

The reins are held between the third and little fingers and between thumb and forefinger. Wrists should be slightly rounded, with fingers closed around the reins and with thumbs on top. If your hands are held correctly, you will be able to see your finger-nails facing towards you. Some people ride with their hands like dogs paws, with knuckles uppermost. This is incorrect because it does not allow any elasticity in your contact with the horse; and hands therefore become very hard. If the hands are held correctly, there will be some elasticity through the wrists.

A straight line from the rider's shoulder, through the hip to the back of the heel, shows that the leg is in the right position. I like to ride with my leg on the horse the whole time. Some people think that means having the leg clamped

on, whereas it should be a fairly loose contact from the lower leg. The foot should be parallel with the horse's side, with the weight well down in the heel.

Basic aids

The first thing the horse has to be taught is his response to the basic aids. When you use your legs he must go forward; when you use your hands he must stop. Although this sounds very simple, it's amazing the number of people who neglect to train their horses to respond to these two basic requirements.

You should not have to keep kicking the horse. If he fails to walk forward with normal pressure, you will have to back up the leg aid with a stick or spurs. Then, when you ask again with normal pressure, he should learn to move forward straight away. If he fails to do so, you need to repeat the exercise more firmly.

When you first start educating the horse to be responsive to the leg aids, he should have complete freedom of his head with no contact on the reins. Once he has learnt to move forward for the legs, the hands should maintain a light contact with the horse's mouth while he does so. It must not be a restrictive contact, otherwise you would have a conflict of aids with the horse being asked to move forward and stop at the same time.

When moving from halt to walk, you should apply an even pressure with both legs just behind the girth. At the same time you should relax your arms in order to allow the horse to move forward, while still keeping a light contact on the reins. The same aids are applied for the transition from walk to trot.

In downward transitions, the horse must learn to respond to your hands; if he fails to do so, you have to be firm in order to establish the aid in his mind. Once he does stop or slow down to the required pace, you should release the weight on the reins immediately. He will soon realise that this is his reward for responding to the hand.

He should learn to stop as soon as you ask him, which may take a few training sessions to achieve. If you let the horse dribble on for a few

The horse is being worked in an overbent outline in training to make his whole shape more rounded. This would not be a correct outline for the dressage test.

Having been asked to raise his shoulder and outline, the horse has come up a little too high and is showing some tension.

The horse is now showing a very good outline in trot, which would help him to get high marks in a dressage test. He has been plaited (braided) in order to train his mane to stay on one side.

Riding without stirrups. I have let my shoulders collapse, which shows how easy it is to get into bad habits.

strides before coming to a halt, he will continue to do the same thing. Since training always begins with the slower paces, downward transitions would start with walk to halt and trot to walk.

I like to train the horse to come back not only for the hand but for the body as well. This is achieved by sitting up a little and, as it were, holding him with your back. At the same time you should put your weight slightly back, close the thighs, while keeping a light contact with the lower leg, and resist with the hands. There should be no pulling back; it is more a question of closing your hands around the reins than taking a physical pull.

Contact

Whether you are training a novice or re-schooling an older horse that needs to go back to basics, you will be aiming to establish contact between the leg and hand. The horse has to accept this contact before you can get him into an outline and going forward in a rhythm. He will not learn anything by being ridden on a slack rein. He needs to be on the bit, which is a very loose term

that means different things according to the level of training. With an untrained horse, it means no more than accepting the hand with a light contact and going in an outline, albeit one that is fairly long and low.

Points for the rider

One of the most common errors is for people to ride completely on the hand. Getting the horse on the bit is not a question of winching its head in; he has to work from the rider's leg into the hand. This is one of the essential basics of correct schooling; without it the horse will be incapable of doing more advanced work. You can never expect the horse to go in the correct way if he is not ridden correctly.

Most problems occur because people fail to ride from the leg. They do not appreciate that in order to get the horse correctly on the bit, so that he maintains a light contact, he has to work forward from the leg into the hand. The novice rider will almost certainly need help in this early stage of the horse's education because it will have such a big influence on the rest of his training. I have seen horses that were so badly schooled that

The horse is showing a good novice outline at sitting trot.

you would end up needing Reiner Klimke, the great dressage trainer from Germany, to get them going correctly on the bit!

Riders should remember that doing exercises to improve the horse is only one part of the training programme; there are plenty of things they can do to make themselves better. Riding without stirrups on or off the lunge will help to make you more secure in the saddle which, in turn, will make it easier for you to use your legs correctly. It will also help you to acquire an independent seat, which is vital. Without it, you will never succeed in riding with a still hand.

Rising trot without stirrups is an effective way of strengthening the leg muscles. You can do it for one minute, then sit again before doing it for another minute, gradually building up as the muscles grow stronger. General fitness exercises, such as skipping, cycling, squash and running, will also help. So will any type of gym work, especially exercises that strengthen the back and legs.

Novice riders often find it difficult to use different parts of their bodies independently of each other; this is something that has to be learnt

through training. When giving lessons, I often find that the riders' arms or hands tense up or start flapping as soon as they are asked to use their legs. The more still and relaxed you can be in your seat and hands, the better chance the horse will have of understanding the aids and making smooth transitions.

If you run into problems, do get help. Napping, for example, is something that needs to be dealt with immediately, otherwise the horse knows that it has the measure of its rider and misbehaves all the more. If any horse in my yard started napping, I would be tough on it from the beginning. It may only require one whack of the stick, followed by very positive aids to move forward, to straighten the horse out. Obviously the circumstances have to be taken into account; it would be dangerous to adopt these tactics on busy or slippery roads. Having said that, napping can be a dangerous vice in itself.

Horses have been cured of napping by using their boredom threshold as a weapon. A typical instance is when the horse stops dead in its tracks and refuses to move forward another inch. In theory, you make him stand there for as long as it

takes, until he is so bored that he consents to move in the only direction that you allow, which is forwards. In practice, he is unlikely to stand still; he will probably try to whip round and he may rear. If you are not a strong enough rider to cope, then get help from someone who is capable of nipping the problem in the bud.

Walk and trot

The rider needs to learn the correct speed for each of the horse's basic paces. At walk he should be moving forward in an active, brisk and fairly free sort of way — a bit like most horses when they are walking home to their stables. Some riders tend to hang onto the horse's head too much, which keeps the neck too short. This means that the horse is prevented from using its shoulder properly, so it cannot stretch forward and have a good walk. I like to encourage my pupils to relax the arm and ride forward in walk, rather than let the horse dawdle along.

A good example of lengthening stride in trot, showing all four feet suspended off the ground. If anything, I would like the horse's neck to be a little longer, but the strides are correct, with the back legs covering the same distance as the front legs.

The trot should be an active, working trot. The tendency here is for the riders to go too slowly, so that the horse is almost jogging. Having said that, it is just as bad to go flat out. Quite often, novice riders need someone to tell them how fast to go in working trot — which may mean going a bit faster or, if the horse is moving quickly and tending to lose its balance, slowing down a little. Once the horse learns to balance itself and work more on its hocks, the trot steps can show considerable improvement.

Canter

Before asking the horse to canter, you should make sure that he is willing to go forward in trot and that you don't have to kick him all the time

The horse has become high and against the hand in canter.

to keep him moving. The easiest way to teach the strike-off to canter is on a large circle, as this will encourage the horse to lead with the correct leg. He should be bent between the rider's inside leg (which, together with the inside rein, creates the bend) and the outside rein (which controls the outside shoulder and the amount of bend).

The aid to canter should be given from sitting trot, but you need to avoid asking for the transition too soon. If you ask for canter as soon as you sit to the trot, the horse will begin to think that it is part of the aid. That could lead to him striking off into canter every time you begin sitting trot. You should give yourself time to make sure he is balanced and going forward in sitting trot and then apply the aid.

For canter to the left, you need to put your weight on your left seat-bone while using the inside (left) leg just behind the girth and the outside (right) leg further back. The left hand asks the horse to bend to the left as he moves forward on the circle, while the right hand gives enough to allow for the correct bend but still maintains a firm contact. It may be necessary to apply the leg aids quite strongly when you are first teaching the horse to canter but, once he understands what they mean, you should not need to use a lot of pressure.

Some riders make the mistake of trying to throw the horse into canter. They do this by throwing the upper part of the body forward and leaning to the inside, which only serves to unbalance the horse. If you lean to the left you will put all your weight on the horse's left shoulder and he will have to change his balance to compensate. He may strike off on the wrong leg as a result.

There should be no kicking and flapping, with the horse trotting at full speed and then lurching into canter. If you can't get a strike-off within

Here I am asking for exaggerated right flexion to soften the horse and get him to give to the right rein. Note that I am giving support from my right leg and that I still have contact with the left rein.

three or four strides of asking, you should come back to a nice, balanced trot and then ask again. If that doesn't work you may need to back up the leg aids with the stick or spurs, so that the horse learns that you are telling him to go forward into canter. Then repeat the normal aids again to see if the message has struck home.

If I had trouble getting a young horse into canter, I would get him to do it without bothering about which leg he was on. Once he has learnt to strike-off without first going into fast trot (which means I need to keep some contact to stop him running on), I can start being more particular. I would not canter many circles; it is better to come back to trot and ask again, repeating the process on both reins until the horse understands.

In the beginning the canter might need to be a little long and fast if the horse is young and not naturally well-balanced. You have to learn to put up with that, letting the canter go further forward than you want it to. The horse will learn to balance itself faster than he would if you had a big fight about getting him to canter at the speed you want. Once he finds his balance at the faster canter, you can start to ask him to slow down and become a little more collected. Initially, you might need to be quite firm with your hands and legs in order to let him know that you want a slower canter.

Before asking the horse to come back to trot, the rider has to slow and balance the canter as much as possible. If the horse falls onto his forehand and then runs away in trot, the rider should immediately bring the horse back to the correct speed before softening the hand again.

Schooling sessions

There are plenty of shapes that you can follow, which will help improve the horse's balance. These include circles of varying sizes, squares, half-circles, serpentines and figures-of-eight. I always start each one at walk before progressing to trot and canter. Walk is the easiest pace for a young horse when he is learning new things; it is also easier for the rider to correct mistakes while the horse is walking.

The horse should maintain contact, outline and rhythm during these exercises, which would also include transitions within the shapes. You will help to keep the horse's attention by asking him for a variety of things: different shapes and paces; transitions; a change of rein.

Riding the horse in trot on a large 20 m (65 ft) circle, followed by a smaller 10 m (32 ft) circle will encourage him to balance and use himself properly. In canter, I would decrease the size of the circle more gradually — maybe from 20 m (65 ft) to 15 m (49 ft), 12 m (39 ft) and 10 m

(32 ft). Throughout these exercises, the horse will need to maintain the correct bend on the circle, which is achieved by riding him from the inside leg into the outside hand. He also needs to work on both reins.

When riding squares (again on both reins) you are constantly asking the horse to straighten up, turn and straighten up again, which makes it a useful exercise. Starting at walk, you should try to maintain the horse's rhythm on the square; he should not be allowed to start creeping.

As you reach each corner of a square to the left, you should bring your left hand away from the horse's neck, making it very clear that you want him to bend and turn in that direction. You should use your inside (left) leg just behind the girth to stop him falling in, with support from your outside (right) hand and leg, which is used further back to control the horse's quarters. During this exercise, you should think about

The horse is stretching down and forward, while still maintaining a light contact with the rein.

keeping the horse's shoulders in front of you and parallel with your own. It will help you to use whatever aid is necessary to achieve straightness.

These exercises can be hard work for the horse, so he should not be given 20 minutes of solid drilling. He needs the chance to relax every so often, stretching his neck out for a minute or two to give his muscles a rest. If he finds training uncomfortable, he will become argumentative about doing it.

Transitions

More than anything else, I believe in practising transitions. They help to balance the horse and keep him listening, whether they have shortening and lengthening strides within the paces or a change from one pace to another. I would start by asking for simple transitions, such as walk to trot and trot to walk. Then I would work on trot to canter and back down to trot again. It is all

part of teaching the horse to progress from those simple, basic aids of going forward for the leg and stopping for the hand.

I will also be working on transitions within each pace. At trot, for example, I might ask for a few lengthened strides before coming back to working trot. Once the transitions are correct, I find that the rest of the work improves, including the paces. I am also aware that we will earn higher marks in the dressage phase of the events if the horse's transitions are smooth and accurate.

The half-halt

All our horses are taught the half-halt, which is useful as a preparation for transitions. It also helps to balance the horse and attract his attention, making him more receptive to the rider.

Here the horse is stretched forward and down through his neck on a long rein.

The horse has to learn the half-halt gradually, through transitions from trot to three or four strides of walk and then back to trot again. The walk strides can then be decreased and finally omitted, so that the horse is momentarily slowing the pace in trot and then going forward again. While doing so, it is important that he should maintain an outline.

The aids for the half-halt, which can be used in all three basic paces, are the same as those in downward transitions. The rider should sit up and keep the weight slightly back, while closing with the thighs and resisting with the hands. As soon as the horse slows the pace, the arms should relax to let him go forward again. Eventually, as he becomes more educated, he will respond just

Again in canter, but this time the horse is rounder and working through the hand.

to the change in weight. As training progresses, the half-halt will help to create more impulsion through the horse momentarily collecting and shortening himself.

Other priorities

The horse should always be kept in a round outline; he must not be allowed to go hollow. He must also stay straight, which means that his hind feet have to follow in the same track as his forefeet, except in lateral movements. His body must therefore be straight when moving forward in a straight line, and curved when going in a circle. All of which brings me back to emphasising the necessity of working the horse from the leg into the hand; you cannot achieve straightness and a nice, round outline otherwise.

As already mentioned, I like to vary the exercises. There is nothing more boring for horse or

41

rider than doing the same thing over and over again. It is good to ask the horse for little things that are new to him because he will learn more that way. At the same time, you must be aware of how much he understands and make sure that you don't confuse him. If he gets upset or starts to panic about his work, it is better to go back to things that have already been established. Once his confidence is restored, you can ask him for a little bit more again.

Work on the flat has to take account of the horse's individual strengths and weaknesses. Some are obviously going to prove more difficult than others. I remember the time and patience required when schooling Face the Music, a horse I won with at Burghley. He had a very difficult temperament and, instead of my usual policy of keeping the lessons varied, I ended up doing a lot of slow and repetitive work. It was intensely boring but it had the required effect of quietening him down.

Leg-yield

This movement, which is initially taught at walk, is the start of the horse's lateral work. It teaches him to move forwards and sideways, away from the rider's leg, and it encourages him to bring his inside hind leg further under his body. He will therefore carry more weight on that leg, which helps his hocks to become engaged. This, in

turn, will make it easier for him to perform more difficult movements later in his education.

Leg-yield requires the horse to move diagonally, with his neck slightly flexed in the opposite direction to the way he is moving. This means that if you are riding leg-yield to the left, you should just be able to see the horse's right eye. The horse's body should stay parallel to the side of the arena, or to a fence at the side of a field, while he moves forwards and sideways, crossing his legs over as he goes.

Assuming that I was working in an arena, I would start the movement from the centre line. First, I would make sure that the horse was straight, then (if riding leg-yield to the left) I would put more weight on my right seat-bone and ask the horse to move away from my right leg. The weight should be well down on the heel, with the right (inside) leg pressed against the horse just behind the girth. If the pressure is too far back you would be asking him to move his hindquarters over, which is not the object of the exercise.

The left leg, used a little further back, maintains the impulsion. The right hand asks for a slight flexion in the neck, while the left hand controls the degree of bend and stops the horse falling out through his left shoulder. Unless it is necessary in the initial training, you should not move the left hand away from the horse; the rein should lie flat along its neck. You should also be careful to maintain the correct position yourself. It is all too easy for riders to collapse a hip and drop a shoulder during this exercise.

When you introduce leg-yield to the horse, he may not understand that he is being asked to move diagonally away from your leg and he will probably try to go faster. Having let him know with the hands that this is not what you require, you have to ask again with the leg for him to move sideways.

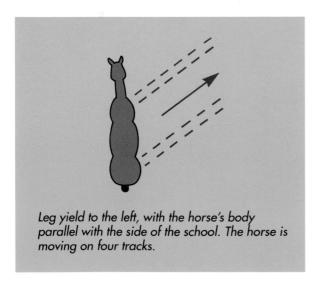

Leg yield to the left, with the horse's body parallel with the side of the school. The horse is moving on four tracks.

Opposite: *Leg-yield to the left, with the horse showing almost too much bend to the right.*

At this stage you may find it helpful to move your left hand away from the horse to show him the direction you want him to go. If he fails to respond, you may have to use the stick or spur as a back-up to your right leg to help him understand the aid. If the horse is not performing the movement properly, you should immediately correct his position and ask again.

Riders often ask too much too soon. Initially I am only concerned with teaching the horse to move away from my leg; I am not worried about whether or not his head is in the air. When he does understand, you can ask him to leg-yield to left and right while staying in a rounded outline with his head in the correct place. Once he is happy to respond to the aids in walk, he can progress to trot. But, as in all new exercises, you should avoid doing too much on one day. Horses, like people, get stiff and sore when asked to use new muscles, so these exercises need to be introduced gradually.

Shoulder-in

This is the next lateral movement for the horse to learn and it, too, should be introduced gradually. It requires the horse to move forward with his shoulders off the track, while his hind legs stay on it. He should always be bent correctly around your inside leg.

Before attempting a proper shoulder-in, you may find it helpful simply to ask the horse to maintain a flexion towards the centre of the school or field, without moving his shoulders off the track, for maybe six to ten strides. Once he can manage that a couple of times, you can ask him for the real thing — but without looking for much angle and bend to begin with.

Shoulder-in to the left would begin with a 10 m (32 ft) circle to the left to ensure that your horse is correctly bent between the inside (left) leg and the outside (right) hand. As he completes the circle, you need to increase the contact with the

Shoulder-in to the left. This clearly shows the horse moving on three tracks. He is on the correct angle, but could show a little more bend to the left.

Shoulder-in to the left, with the horse moving on three tracks.

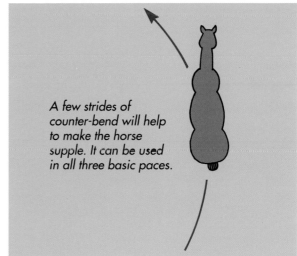

A few strides of counter-bend will help to make the horse supple. It can be used in all three basic paces.

outside rein to bring the horse's shoulders off the track. It is a big mistake for the rider to pull his shoulders off it with the inside rein.

At the same time you should keep your weight on the left seat-bone and, using the left leg just behind the girth, ask the horse to move along the track. It is vitally important that he should maintain his track along the side of the school from the inside (left) leg. The left rein asks for a bend to the left and is occasionally used to support the left leg. It should not be crossed over the withers, as this would have the effect of twisting the horse's neck, producing an incorrect shoulder-in. The bend should come mainly from the left leg. The right leg (used just behind the girth) maintains the impulsion and can also be used to correct the position of the quarters if necessary.

The idea of shoulder-in is to encourage the horse to bring his inside hind leg further under his body, thereby helping to achieve the long-term aim of greater impulsion. This can only be obtained if ridden correctly. Your shoulders should be turned in the direction of the horse and you should try to avoid the common mistake of collapsing the left hip.

Hacking

To be fit for the events, the horse will need to be ridden most days for an hour or so. Since the schooling sessions last for 20 minutes at most,

the rest of his exercise is normally taken out hacking. This is good for him because it gets him out and about where he can see different things. If the horse spends most of his time in the school, he can begin to wonder what has struck him when suddenly confronted with wide open spaces.

While out hacking, you can do many of the things that you were practising in the school or field — transitions, maybe a little leg-yield, possibly a five-minute stretch when you ask him to come on the bit and pay attention. The hack should not be too regimented. I believe that the horse should be allowed to go out and have some enjoyment, but you are not going to ruin his pleasure by occasionally asking him for something extra.

Methods and aims

Training horses is basically done through repetition. They do not think logically, so we have to train them on a system of reward and correction. When they do as you ask you should reward them with a pat. When they do something badly (or not at all) you have to ask again a little more strongly. It is very important that the horse should be corrected immediately when he does something wrong. That doesn't mean getting rough with him; you only confuse the horse if you try to bully him. Instead you need to come back to what you were doing before, re-position the horse and ask again.

The novice dressage test is not demanding. If the horse is trained to walk, trot and canter when asked to do so, the test should not be a problem. At this stage I would be looking for him to stay in his outline, keep his rhythm, stay straight and perform transitions obediently.

The horse is now showing better bend during shoulder-in to the left. The picture shows his inside hind leg coming under his body to make him more engaged.

It is unlikely that I would have achieved all this, but they are the basic aims for a novice event horse. I am not looking for much impulsion before his first event and I am aware that neither his halts nor his lengthening strides at trot are likely to be fantastic. I would want the horse to go forward and show a little lengthening in the strides, but I am not expecting too much in the first few tests. The important thing is to get the basic groundwork firmly established so that you have something to build on for the future.

Summary

Points for the rider
- Always ride from the legs into the hands
- Plan each training session in advance
- Get help from a capable trainer if you are a novice
- Do exercises (e.g., riding without stirrups)
- Learn correct speeds for the basic paces
- Keep the lessons varied
- Practise transitions frequently
- Allow the horse to relax and stretch occasionally during training

The horse must learn to
- Go forward when you use your legs
- Stop or slow down when you use your hands
- Accept contact with your hands and legs
- Maintain a round outline
- Stay straight
- Be correctly bent on a circle, between rider's inside leg and outside hand

Aids
- Upward transitions (halt to walk, walk to trot)
- Keep an even pressure with both legs just behind the girth
- Relax arm
- Keep light contact on reins

- Downward transitions (walk to halt, trot to walk, canter to trot)
- Sit up, with weight slightly back
- Keep active contact with lower leg
- Resist with hands

- Turn to left and canter (left leg leading)
- Weight on left seat-bone
- Left (inside) leg just behind the girth
- Right (outside) leg further back
- Left hand asks for bend to the left
- Right hand allows for correct bend while maintaining firm contact

Half-halt
- Sit up, with weight slightly back
- Close the thighs
- Resist with hands
- Soften hands when horse slows down
- Ride forward out of half-halt

Leg-yield to left
- Weight on right seat-bone
- Right (inside) leg just behind the girth asks horse to move away from it
- Left (outside) leg a little further back maintains impulsion
- Right hand asks for a slight flexion
- Left hand controls degree of flexion and stops horse falling out

Shoulder-in to left
- Weight on left seat-bone
- Left (inside leg) just behind the girth asks horse to move along the track
- Right (outside) leg just behind the girth maintains impulsion
- Left hand asks for bend to the left
- Right rein controls the shoulders

Chapter 4

TRAINING OVER FENCES

By the time one of my horses has its first jump in the school, it would be well used to trotting over poles on the ground. I would have had several scattered around the school while working on the flat. The horse will have gone over them, first in walk and, once he was happy doing that, in trot.

I might also use trotting poles in a line, set 1–1.4 m (3½–4½ ft) apart, for the horse to trot over. In the process he soon begins to learn that going over poles is no big deal and therefore nothing to get excited about. It is essential that the horse maintains the rhythm of the trot during these exercises which teach him, among other things, to look where he is going and pick up his feet.

The horse may also have learnt to jump a few natural obstacles while out hacking. If I come across a little log, for instance, I would trot over it. Young horses find it far more natural to jump that sort of obstacle than coloured poles in the school, and I think they take to it more easily.

Having said that, I have taught plenty of horses to take their first jump over coloured poles.

Rider's position

The obvious change in position between flat work and jumping is that the stirrup leathers are shorter. I normally put mine up by about four holes, but I have very long legs and I also ride quite long on the flat, so there is a big difference between my stirrup lengths. Most riders would probably only shorten the leathers by two holes; if they have very short legs, maybe by only one. The length of the stirrups should allow you to bring your seat out of the saddle, but still be long enough for your lower leg to be in contact with the horse.

Apart from the knees being higher, the leg

Above: *Cantering over poles on the ground is a useful exercise for teaching obedience, rhythm and balance.*
Opposite: *A horse showing exuberance over a low fence.*

Once you are confident cantering over poles on the ground, you can add a small jump to the two canter poles, which will encourage the horse to keep his rhythm.

position is much the same as in flat work, with the weight well down in the heel. The knees should not be turned in like a gripping device; that would mean a loss of contact because it would cause the lower leg to move away from the horse. The upper body should be tilted slightly forward from the hip and, as a result of that, the reins will be a little shorter.

First jumping lessons

Once the horse is trotting (and, possibly, cantering) over scattered poles on the ground, I like to teach it to jump fairly soon. I always start off with a little cross-pole, maybe with a few trotting poles in front of it. These should be 1–1.4 m (3½–4½ ft) apart, leaving a distance of 2.5–2.8 m (8–9 ft) between the last pole and the jump.

The poles are a good idea for inexperienced riders. They make the horse concentrate and prevent any tendency that he (or the rider) may have to rush at the fence. Rushing is invariably caused by bad training, so you need to be careful to discourage it. That means resisting any temptation you might have to give the horse an extra kick, before throwing yourself forward, lifting your hands as though pulling him off the ground and simultaneously shouting 'Hup'! All that effectively does is put the horse off balance and make his job more difficult. As well as trying to get over the obstacle, he has to compensate for the rider moving out of balance and for being yanked in the mouth. The more you can keep still with the hands and upper body, just giving support from the lower leg, the better the horse will jump.

As the horse trots into the fence, the rider should be concentrating on staying in balance with him, keeping him straight and in rhythm, and giving him support from hand and leg. I like young horses to use their own initiative as much

as possible, so I would not dictate the right place for take-off. When the rider interferes too much, the horse is unable to use his own judgement and you can start to run into problems as a result. Although he should be trained to listen to the rider, he must also learn how to look after himself.

Assuming the horse has some intelligence, he is quick to learn by his own mistakes. If he were to trot into the fence, more or less flop over it

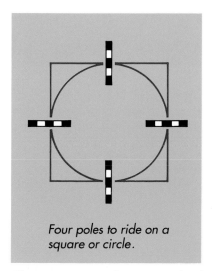

Four poles to ride on a square or circle.

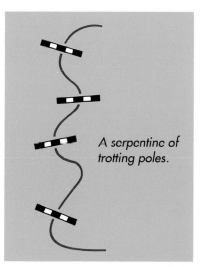

A serpentine of trotting poles.

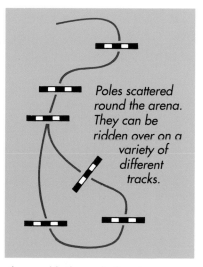

Poles scattered round the arena. They can be ridden over on a variety of different tracks.

Three exercises with trotting poles that can be used to improve the horse's rhythm and balance before he starts jumping.

1

2

Having approached in trot, Carolyn goes over a one-stride double with a placing pole before the first fence, another between the two obstacles, and another after the second part of the double.

3

4

The position of her upper body and lower leg is very good and it remains the same throughout the sequence.

5

6

and land in a heap the first time he tried it, he would normally get the message that he has to make a proper jump at the next attempt. If not, he may need a tap from the stick just behind your leg on take-off.

Once the horse is popping happily over the cross-pole, you can remove the trotting poles (possibly leaving the last one as a place pole) and go over it again from trot. Initially, I do most of the early jumping from trot; it gives the rider more control and helps to prevent the problem of rushing. Having jumped the little cross-pole a few more times, I might decide to trot into the fence again and this time canter away from it.

After that I would probably put a second cross-pole two or three strides later. As before, I would trot into the first fence and land over it in canter; the horse would then take the requisite number of strides to jump the second element. This is a good way of introducing the horse to jumping from canter.

Grids

From there you can build up to various grids, like the examples shown in the diagrams. These should help the horse to build up confidence; the stridings are worked out for him so that he arrives at the right place to take off for each fence. It is easier for both horse and rider to jump an obstacle as part of a grid than it would be if it were out on its own. Grids are a very good gymnastic exercise for training the horse in jumping.

At first the grids should be designed to make the job as easy as possible for the horse. If he had a big, long stride, you would need to lengthen the distance to make it more comfortable for him. By the same token, if he were a small, short-striding horse you would need to reduce the distances a little, otherwise you would probably have to chase him through the grid and so encourage him to rush.

At a later stage in his education, I would use distances within the grid to encourage the horse to shorten or lengthen his stride. But, initially, I would be concentrating solely on the jump. It is a mistake to try doing too many things at once.

Regular schooling

I usually jump the baby novices almost every day that I school them. It becomes part of their lessons and, as in the flat work, involves trying to teach them something each time.

I would possibly trot over half a dozen fences or go down a grid two or three times. If you only jump the horse once a week he is not going to learn very fast; if he does a little bit every day the progress will be much quicker.

I would never jump the same grid day in and day out. There are endless ways of changing it, for example, by varying the number of strides between the elements or the striding sequence, so that the horse keeps learning new things.

Running-out and refusing

I like to use poles on the fences as wings. These help young horses to concentrate and stay straight, as well as discouraging them from running-out, which is definitely something to be avoided.

Having said that, it can sometimes happen. If it does, I would immediately tell the horse that he has done something wrong — first by stopping him, then by turning him round with a firm kick in the opposite direction to the way he was going. In other words, if he dodges out to the left you should turn him to the right and then come back and present him to the fence again. He should not be allowed to continue on a left-handed circle as this would suggest that he has gained the upper hand.

If the horse runs out or refuses, he has to be told that he has done something wrong — which does not mean beating him up or getting rough with him. You simply need to be firm, so that he learns that this is something he is not supposed to do. If the rider pats the horse and says 'never mind', he will learn straight away that this is acceptable behaviour.

Seeing the stride

Learning to see a stride is mainly a question of practice. The best method is to put up a small

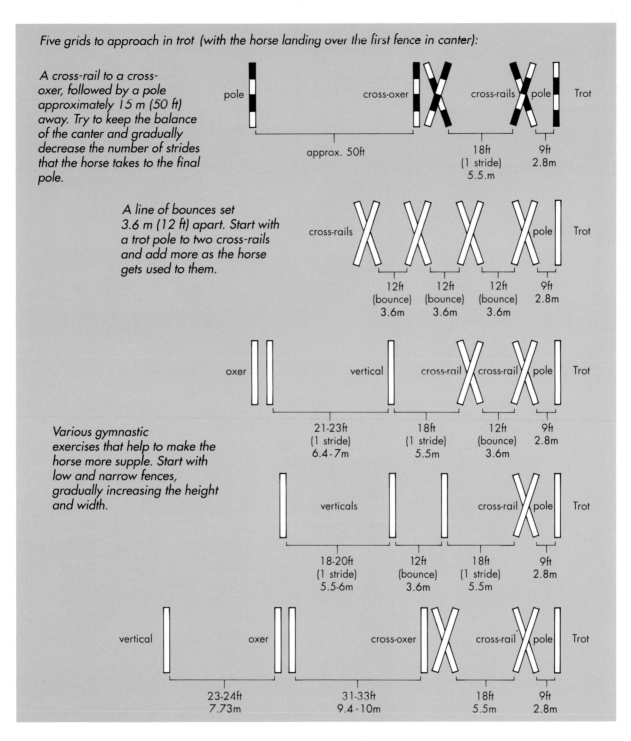

Five grids to approach in trot (with the horse landing over the first fence in canter):

A cross-rail to a cross-oxer, followed by a pole approximately 15 m (50 ft) away. Try to keep the balance of the canter and gradually decrease the number of strides that the horse takes to the final pole.

pole · cross-oxer · cross-rails · pole · Trot

approx. 50ft

18ft
(1 stride)
5.5.m

9ft
2.8m

A line of bounces set 3.6 m (12 ft) apart. Start with a trot pole to two cross-rails and add more as the horse gets used to them.

cross-rails · pole · Trot

12ft
(bounce)
3.6m

12ft
(bounce)
3.6m

12ft
(bounce)
3.6m

9ft
2.8m

oxer · vertical · cross-rail · cross-rail · pole · Trot

21-23ft
(1 stride)
6.4-7m

18ft
(1 stride)
5.5m

12ft
(bounce)
3.6m

9ft
2.8m

Various gymnastic exercises that help to make the horse more supple. Start with low and narrow fences, gradually increasing the height and width.

verticals · cross-rail · pole · Trot

18-20ft
(1 stride)
5.5-6m

12ft
(bounce)
3.6m

18ft
(1 stride)
5.5m

9ft
2.8m

vertical · oxer · cross-oxer · cross-rail · pole · Trot

23-24ft
7.73m

31-33ft
9.4-10m

18ft
5.5m

9ft
2.8m

fence on its own and then ride round to it on a large circle, keeping the horse in a rhythm. You should not attempt to make any adjustments; the horse should be left to his own devices at the obstacle while you concentrate on keeping him to a steady, balanced canter. Eventually you should learn to see whether or not the horse is going to be on the right stride — and what to do about it when you see that the stride is wrong. This may mean asking the horse to shorten, or you may want to put more leg on and ask him to lengthen.

1

2

3

4

Another one-stride double with placing poles. One pole has been set 2.5–2.8 m (8–9 ft) before the first fence, another equidistant between the two elements, and a third 2.5–2.8 m (8–9 ft) beyond the second fence. The poles help the horse to keep its rhythm through the line. They also encourage him to keep looking, stretching his head and neck down to make a rounder shape as he jumps.

A low fence followed by one stride to an oxer. The horse goes over a placing pole while making the one canter stride.

I think people get in too much of a state about not being able to see a stride. It would be far more profitable for them to concentrate on keeping a rhythm to the fence and to avoid interfering with the horse when he jumps it. Some riders have the horse practically jumping up and down on the spot while they look for a stride, which achieves nothing. It simply upsets the horse's balance and rhythm. If he is coming into the fence on a regular rhythm, you have far more chance of seeing a stride than when he is constantly shortening and lengthening.

Another pole has been placed beyond the oxer to encourage this particular horse to jump out and over it.

Gaining confidence

The rate of progress — and the size of the fences — will depend on the individual horse and the competence of the rider. If you lack confidence, it obviously makes sense to keep the fences low until you feel safe jumping them. Once you can ride with assurance into a 75 cm (2 ft 6 in) fence in a rhythm, and, maybe, make a small adjustment if the stride is wrong, you should be ready to build up the same confidence at 90 cm (3 ft) and then at 1 m (3 ft 6 in).

Some horses are natural jumpers; they want to

The horse is showing a good shape over a vertical jump of planks. We have moved a pole away from the base to give a ground-line, which helps him to use his natural technique effectively.

go over the fence in a nice way and clear it. I have one called Regal Scot, who proved an absolute natural from day one. Thoroughbreds are not always like that; they are bred to race rather than jump and they can often take a little longer to train over fences. You would expect to get quicker results with one of the warm-blood, show-jumping types that are bred in a lot of European countries, such as Germany, the Netherlands, Belgium and Sweden. They have jumping in their blood and they normally take to it straight away.

When the horse is jumping happily through grids and over single fences, I would set up a mini-course for him. I don't have enough jumps to put up a proper course at home, but I can set up a double and two or three other fences. If these are built so that they can be jumped in either direction, I have plenty of options and various different lines to take. If I had sufficient time (which is rarely the case) I would also take the horse to a few little jumping shows before he competes in his first one-day event.

Cross-country-type fences

The horse would also be introduced to some of the components of cross-country fences while playing around in the school. I would teach him to jump single fences on an angle and then, maybe, set up small obstacles on different angles and ask him to keep a straight line over them. I would also use two rails to build a very small corner, which would be similar to jumping at the side of a small oxer. As the horse gains confidence, the angle can gradually be made wider so that he becomes accustomed to jumping corner fences before he tackles a solid cross-country one.

You could use a water tray or even a piece of blue plastic to put down as a mock ditch under a small jump. Then you could build a small fence on either side of it so that you have something resembling a coffin, though without the normal dip between the two fences.

Narrow obstacles can also be practised. One way would be to get two 46-gallon drums and lay them down lengthways. Having trotted backwards and forwards over this obstacle, you could remove one of the drums and put two guide poles on the remaining one. Once the horse is jumping the single drum quite happily, you can ask him to go over it without the poles to guide him.

Dealing with problems

It would be nice to think that you have chosen your horse so wisely that he doesn't present any problems, but that is rarely the case. Most have a few odd little quirks that have to be ironed out. However, there is no doubt that prevention is better than cure. If you can avoid letting the horse refuse, run-out or rush at his fences, you will save yourself much time and effort.

I do a lot of work with poles on the ground, which is particularly helpful if the horse has a tendency to rush. I might put three or four in a line at no special distances; they could be anything from 3 m (10 ft) to 12 m (40 ft) apart. I would first walk the horse over them, making sure that he kept his rhythm and stayed relaxed. Then I would trot over them, again keeping him in a nice, even rhythm as he goes down the line of poles.

Because he has to go over them, the horse equates the poles with jumping and he may want to quicken as he approaches each one. It is up to the rider to say no. If he tries to go faster, you should resist with your hands and tell him that he is not allowed to increase his pace.

The horse should be looking to see where he is going, while trotting in rhythm over the poles. Once he is doing this in a relaxed way, you can start to do transitions within the line. You might trot over one pole, come back to walk over the next one, then move into trot again. Transitions should be varied so that the horse learns to be obedient and listen within that very simple line. You have no need to worry about the poles — the horse is not going to hurt himself if he treads on one — so you can focus all your attention on getting him to go in a rhythmic and relaxed way.

For canter work, I would start with one pole on a circle. The horse must learn to canter over it without altering his rhythm. If he attempts to rush, you will need to hold him with both hands to let him know that this is not allowed. The next stage could be cantering over more poles, maybe two within a line at 6 m (20 ft) apart, so that you have to adjust the horse's speed to fit in the strides while maintaining the rhythm. You can then use the same principle over very low fences. Getting the horse to be obedient at that level will make life much easier when the jumps get bigger.

Summary

- Horse learns to go over trotting poles
- Start jumping over little cross-pole
- Initially jump fences from trot
- Possibly put second cross-pole two or three strides away
- Build up to grids
- Set up a mini-course
- Practise components of cross-country fences (e.g., corners)

Points for the rider
- Keep hands and upper body as still as possible
- Concentrate on staying in balance with the horse
- Keep him straight and in rhythm
- Correct horse if he refuses or runs out
- Do not allow him to rush
- Train yourself to see a stride

Chapter 5
CROSS-COUNTRY SCHOOLING

Few people have cross-country fences to practise on at home, but you can usually find a few natural obstacles when you go hacking. Little logs, ditches and maybe a stream to walk through will all help to educate the horse for cross-country jumping. If he is jumping confidently in the school, I would then arrange to take him to a cross-country training place that had a good variety of fences at the lowest level. I would not consider jumping corners or angles on cross-country fences until the horse was jumping straightforward obstacles with plenty of confidence.

I would want all the obstacles or at least a selection of them to be small enough for the horse to jump easily out of trot, especially if he is very green. He will not have seen anything like this before, so you have to assume that he is going to be a bit spooky. If he does take fright at an obstacle, it will still be possible to make him

go forward and jump it from trot or walk — or even from a standstill. He has to learn that he must go forward and jump the fence once he has been presented to it.

When I go cross-country schooling I always wear a hard hat, back protector and spurs, and I carry a cross-country or jumping whip. My students are expected to do the same. The only possible exception would be the spurs; if the horse was particularly flighty or sensitive, the rider is probably better off without them.

If you and the horse are both novices, it would be a good idea to have someone on a more experienced horse to accompany you for your first cross-country school. If you did run into difficulties, you would then have someone to give you a lead over whichever fence was proving troublesome.

Alternatively, you could have a helper on the

Young horses start their cross-country schooling over natural obstacles, like this little log.

ground with a lunge whip. This could be used to encourage the horse to go forward, maybe over a jump, down a step or into water, if he is reluctant to do so. You need to avoid getting into a situation in which the horse adamantly refuses to go forward and you eventually have to give up and go home. It will mean that the horse has gained the upper hand and that he will almost certainly be more difficult next time.

Rider's position

My stirrup leathers are normally at least two holes shorter than show-jumping length for riding across country. But, as already mentioned, I have very long legs and I probably shorten my stirrups a bit more than most other riders. They need to be shortened because the faster speed of the cross-country means that your centre of balance has to be slightly more forward, with your weight off the horse's back.

However, when introducing a young horse to cross-country obstacles, you would not want to be riding so short that you are likely to lose your balance if he spooks or dives sideways. You need to be very secure with your lower legs so that you can use them effectively and keep your balance.

Riding with your seat out of the saddle requires you to use different muscles, so you need to strengthen them before you compete in a one-day event. Otherwise you will find it difficult to sustain a steady cross-country speed for about a mile without flagging.

It would be a good idea to practise the cross-country position a couple of times a week, possibly while out on a hack or while working the horse in the school or field. You will need to pull your stirrups up to the correct length and then do a few minutes in a forward, cross-country-type canter with your seat out of the saddle. You can also practise sitting up in a more balanced position, which you would need to adopt when coming into a fence. All this will help to get you fit as well as strengthening the muscles used for cross-country riding.

The schooling session

After arriving at the training ground, I like to have a trot around the place so that the horse can get used to its surroundings. This also gives me a chance to have a look at the fences and decide which ones I will jump first. I might choose a few of the easiest ones that can be jumped in sequence. You are not going to help the horse's education if you pick your fences haphazardly, one at a time, and then go flying into them.

The first few fences should be taken from a very controlled trot, which will help you keep the horse straight and on a direct line to the obstacle. If you come in too fast, it is easy for the horse to run off past the fence instead of jumping it, especially if you are on a fairly loose rein. He needs to be steady and secure in the hand as he trots into these little obstacles and pops over them.

When the horse has jumped a few cross-country fences out of a controlled trot, he will usually get the hang of it, even if he does have a tendency to be spooky. Different obstacles can then be introduced one at a time. Once he is trotting happily over them, I would go into a steady canter and jump them again, a few at a time.

I would possibly finish off by jumping a course made up of all the fences that the horse had already been over. This involves some repetition and, because the horse had already seen all the obstacles, I would hope that he is happy to canter round in a calm, confident way and jump over them.

With a young horse, the rider should maintain a slightly defensive position, which means that your body weight should not be allowed to get too far forward when approaching the fence. You always have to be thinking that the horse might stop. This should make you ride each fence more positively, with your leg well on, until you feel that you can trust him to jump the fences.

If the horse does spook, you need to be firm. It's no good thinking that the poor thing is new to cross-country jumping and can therefore be allowed to do as he pleases. It's fine if he wants to take a look at the fence, but you should not allow

Going down a bank is another part of the horse's early education.

it to become an excuse for him to dither too long. Once he has had a look at the fence, I would expect him to go forward and jump it.

If he was still hesitant, I would give him a firm kick; if that didn't work, he would get a slap from the stick and be told to get on with it. I would then come back and jump the same obstacle a second and possibly a third time. Hopefully, he will then jump it without any hesitation.

Most training is a matter of common sense, but it has to be said that there are riders who fail to apply it. Their horses quickly learn that they can run rings around them. If you want an obedient horse, you have to be prepared to correct him with a slap of the stick when necessary, or get a stronger rider to do it for you.

The other prime rule is not to rely on speed to get over a fence. Some people think that the only way to tackle a spooky obstacle is to go full tilt at it, whereas the opposite is true. The faster he goes, the easier it is for the horse to run out or get

This horse was a five-year-old when having his first cross-country schooling. He is jumping these little tyres with confidence out of trot.

away from you. More often than not, a young horse will back off the fence when approaching it at speed. You then run the risk of him landing on a rail and frightening himself. Even when he is progressing to bigger obstacles, it may be better for a young horse to come in at a strong trot. You can then keep him firmly between the leg and hand, while riding in a forward-thinking way.

The horse has to learn, from the very first session, that jumping cross-country fences can be fun. Some take to it like ducks to water, but you nevertheless have to be careful not to over-face them too soon. You also need to avoid jumping too many fences; once the horse gets tired he will begin to think that cross-country jumping is too much like hard work.

Most suitable schooling places would have between 10 and 15 fences that can be used for the horse's first session and I would probably jump them two or three times. Once he is taking

The horse jumped this fence really well when he was first presented to it. Now he is aware of the ditch underneath it and he doesn't want to know. He used scare tactics, such as rearing and trying to run off with me, to avoid the situation. I had to be very strong and determined to prevent him getting away with it. Once he has given in and agreed to go forward, you would think that butter wouldn't melt in his mouth!

them in a confident manner, it makes sense to finish the session so that it ends on a good note.

Riding different fences

Ditches

Many horses are very wary of ditches, so you need to make sure that you start with a narrow one. If the horse does stop and spook, you can then make him jump it from a standstill. Even if the ditch is only narrow, the horse must learn

that he has to go forward and jump it. You may need to go backwards and forwards over it a few times, initially in trot, until the horse is jumping it happily. Then you could put a rail over it, before progressing to slightly bigger ditches. These could later be followed by a coffin-type obstacle, with a rail on either side of the ditch.

You would obviously want to start with a very small coffin-type fence, especially if the horse has a tendency to be spooky at ditches. If you were to

Jumping a little bounce. The horse is too close on take-off and the rider has allowed his weight to go forward too soon. The jump becomes awkward as a result.

A second attempt at the bounce. This time the rider is sitting up and staying more in balance with the horse, who therefore jumps much better.

choose one of the larger ones used at novice level, the chances are that the horse would stop at it, which is the one situation that you should always try to avoid.

Ditches are among the few obstacles that can cause the horse to remain spooky for quite a while and you need to be aware of that. Make sure that you don't ask the horse to jump something too big until he is really confident over the smaller obstacles.

When you do progress to larger ditches, they can be the one exception to the rule against using speed to get you over them. I am not talking about flat-out speed, but of riding very strongly and positively into the obstacle. If you were to gallop at it, the horse is likely to back himself off and he may fail to make the distance. You would then be in serious trouble, because he would have become frightened of ditches.

The strong, positive approach can be used

with discretion: at a ditch on its own; one with a rail over it; a trakener; or an open ditch with a fence on the landing side. It would not apply to coffins which belong in a different category, as they have to be ridden as combination fences.

Water

Horses also tend to be wary of water. They need to get used to walking and trotting into it, before jumping over a small log or down a step into water. I would be very careful to choose one that was completely safe, with no hidden holes beneath the surface to give the horse a fright.

Initially I would ask him to walk in and have a short paddle around, while I patted him to give him encouragement. He would be allowed to sniff at the water and be given time to get used to the feel of it around his legs. If he is relaxed and happy, I might even do a small circle in trot

The horse's first introduction to water. It took several minutes of persuasion before he made his first tentative steps into it. At no stage was the horse allowed to turn away from the water.

before coming out. Then I might trot in two or three times. The horse would not be asked to jump into water until he is happy to trot into it without hesitation.

Water and ditches cause more problems with young horses than any other obstacles, so it is important to be thorough in your training right from the beginning. Even if the horse seems full of confidence, it is worth spending time to educate him properly. If you are a novice rider and you are introducing the horse to water for the first time, it would be sensible to have a helper riding a more experienced horse or on the ground with a lunge whip to back you up.

3

Having a walk in the water and getting a reassuring pat. Note the freedom of the horse's head while still maintaining contact.

1

2

Above: *The horse is much happier the second time around.*

If the horse had initially proved spooky at water, you would be advised to go to two or three places that had different types for him to jump before you compete in a one-day event. You need to be pretty sure that you are not going to have a problem at the competition. If you were to get eliminated at the water jump, you would have to

Below: *Having become used to the water, the horse is quite happy to jump in off a little bank and go out the other side.*

1

2

3

go home without jumping it — and that is a situation you should do your best to avoid.

Downhill and uphill fences

The horse has to be particularly well balanced when jumping downhill fences, because they have the effect of putting a lot of weight on his forehand. The rider has to compensate by keeping the horse's front as light as possible, so that he is not running into the base of the fence. You need to keep your upper body back and your lower leg in a secure position, while maintaining contact with the horse's mouth.

If you approach a downhill fence in the correct

3

Jumping a tiny corner which was too inviting to miss!

position, you will have a better chance of helping the horse to keep his balance when he lands. By contrast, most horses find uphill fences fairly easy to jump, as long as you ride into them very positively with plenty of forward impulsion.

Drop fences

Horses are naturally hesitant about jumping drop fences, especially when they are unable to see where they are going to land. In other words, the horse is likely to view a palisade or a ramp off the edge of a bank with extreme suspicion until he has learnt to trust the rider. Your schooling place should have small fences like this, where you can educate the horse to do blind drops by initially taking them out of trot.

I never like to ride drop fences too fast, because the horse is then likely to over-jump them, especially if he is fairly bold. If he does make a really big jump over a drop fence, he will land very heavily and probably frighten himself. He will then begin to dislike drops and become reluctant to jump them.

The other golden rule is that you should never jump them on an angle, unless it is unavoidable, which is unlikely at novice level. If the horse does leave a leg behind on a drop fence, jumping at an angle would have the effect of flipping him over sideways. A fall would then be virtually inevitable.

Banks and steps

When educating the horse over banks and steps, you need to start off with very small obstacles so that he has the chance to learn how to tackle them. Once he gets the message, they are rarely much of a problem. When jumping up a bank or step, you need to stay slightly forward with your weight off the horse's back so that he can get his back-end up. When going down, you need to sit up and help to balance the horse as he jumps off the bank or step.

Combination fences

Jumping cross-country combinations should not be a problem as long as you have practised at home over coloured poles. Little combination fences do not require you to make much of an alteration in your pace, assuming that you are going at a nice, sensible speed.

I nevertheless like to practise slowing down for such obstacles as combinations and drops from an early stage in the horse's education. You should not be slowing down as you come into the obstacle; adjustments have to be made earlier so that you have the horse going forward at the speed you want six strides away from the fence. You will need to learn the correct speed for jumping larger combinations, which depends on the distance between fences.

Corners, angles and narrow fences

Corners can also be practised at home. Some riders have a mental block about jumping them and get over-anxious as a result. This often means that they get their line wrong, leaving the horse with no option but to run out. If you think of it as jumping one side of an oxer, you will be less likely to worry about corners.

You need to educate yourself and the horse over very small obstacles, so that you learn to hold a line and keep a rhythm to corners. Once you can trust the horse not to run out, you will be able to ride him more confidently.

The same applies to jumping angles and narrow fences, such as arrowheads, which should also be practised at home. As long as you start at a simple level and build up slowly, you and the horse should learn to jump them well.

Before the first event

The amount of cross-country schooling you do will obviously depend on the horse's experience and the facilities available. In New Zealand, the horse would probably have been hunting and show-jumping before he went to his first one-day event; he therefore wouldn't need as much schooling as one that was an all-round novice.

In the United States, where the fences are tiny for novice classes, you can substitute the competitions for some of the preparatory schooling. My horses are stabled in England, where there is a wonderful range of facilities for cross-country schooling at every level. I would expect my baby novices to have two or three training sessions before going to their first event. If the rider is inexperienced, it would be a good idea to increase the number of sessions to four or five.

Summary
- Practise over natural obstacles (logs, ditches, etc.)
- Practise cross-country position
- Start schooling session by taking fences from trot
- Be aware that the horse might refuse or run out
- Ride him positively
- If the horse spooks, be firm with him
- Do not rely on speed to get you over fences
- Practise over every type of fence

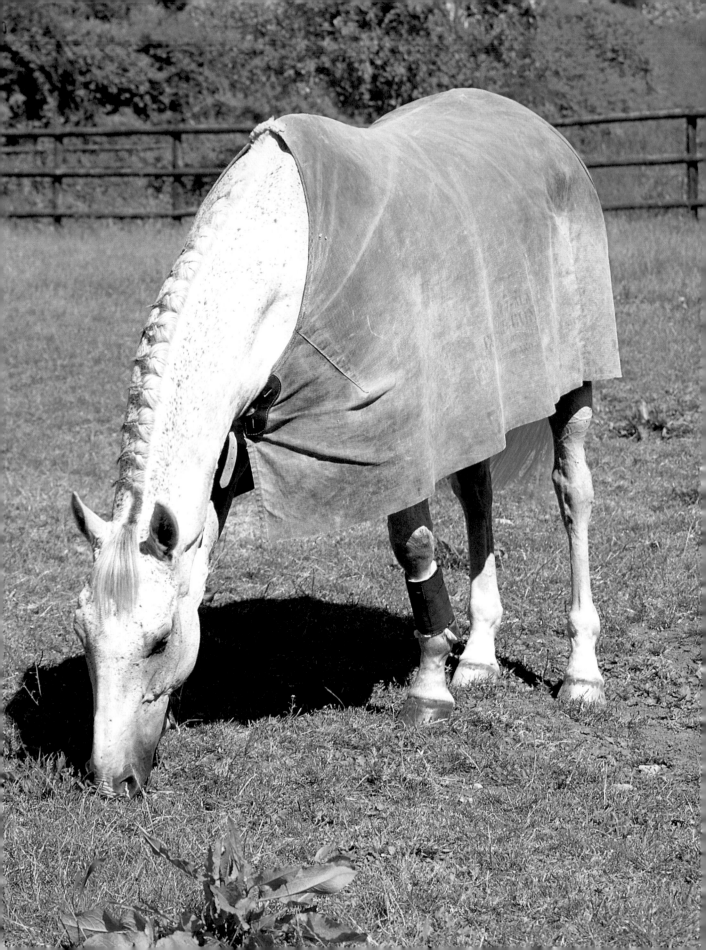

Chapter 6

EQUIPMENT FOR HORSE
AND RIDER

No one can pretend that eventing is a cheap sport, but you certainly don't have to spend a fortune in order to equip yourself and your horse for novice one-day events. Some people do go the whole way and buy every conceivable item of equipment, which makes it unnecessarily expensive.

Some additional items will be needed if you progress to the higher grades of three-day eventing; others will always remain optional extras. There is no point in over-loading yourself with equipment that you do not need, so keep it as simple as possible.

Bitting

Like most riders who have been in the sport for a long time, I have gradually acquired a sizable collection of bits. I always start by giving each horse

Opposite: *Out in the field wearing a New Zealand rug.*

the benefit of the doubt by riding him in a fairly mild bit, probably a loose-ring or eggbutt snaffle. He would stay in one of these (or a mild K-K snaffle) for the dressage, but, if he proved too strong in the show-jumping and cross-country, I would probably change the bit.

I have other snaffle options, such as a French link or a Dr Bristol. If neither of these worked, I might try a vulcanite pelham, which is a particular favourite of mine. I would not automatically look for a stronger bit if I felt that I needed more control. Sometimes a softer bit will prove effective, simply because the horse finds it more comfortable.

The vulcanite pelham was the one that I eventually used with two former partners, Michaelmas Day and Welton Greylag, who were both pullers. We went through a variety of bits with those two horses before deciding that the pelham was the best option. Charisma was also

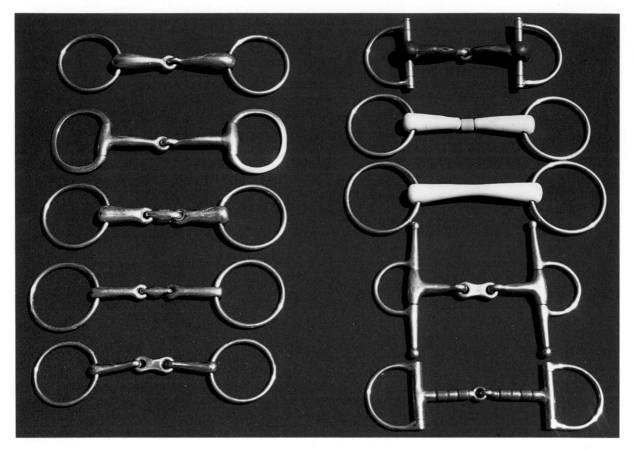

A selection of snaffle bits.
Left from top: plain loose-ring, eggbutt; K-K; K-K with thinner mouthpiece; Dr Bristol.
Right from top: rubber D-ring; loose-ring jointed Nathe (Happy Mouth); straight-mouth Nathe (Happy Mouth); eggbutt Dr Bristol with cheeks; D-ring with copper rollers.

quite strong, but it was sufficient to change him from a rubber snaffle to a thin bridoon to have control. This can quite often happen when you change from a thicker to a thinner bit of the same type.

If your horse tends to go charging off, it might be worth checking his teeth to make sure that they are not the cause of the problem. You should also check that your training and riding are correct before you think about changing the bit. Some riders tend to rev up their horses and unwittingly make them stronger; others switch them off and make them more relaxed, which usually means that they are less difficult to hold. If the horse is quite strong, the rider should learn to sit very quietly (particularly with the leg and seat) and avoid being over-active.

Some horses change when they start competing; they can get stronger, or go the other way and become easier to hold. It is difficult to gauge

which is likely to be the case until the horse has done several events. More often than not, he will become keener across country and you may need to change the bit at that stage.

It is obviously essential for you to have control when you are riding across country. If the horse is difficult to hold in canter at home, he will be just as strong, if not more so, at a one-day event. In this case you will need to experiment with other bits (borrowed, if possible, to avoid a big outlay) until you find the right one. You need to choose carefully; if the bit is too strong, the horse will be worried about its mouth and will not want to take up contact and go forward.

Nothing is more frightening — or more fraught with danger — than being completely out of control on a cross-country course. It happened to me years ago when somebody asked me to event their Grade A show-jumper and he literally ran away with me. We didn't come to grief, so I lived to tell the tale, but it was definitely not a pleasant experience.

Unless you have proper control, you will never be able to get fast times across country. Too much will be wasted in having to slow down at every fence to avoid jumping it at a lunatic speed. You should be able to keep the horse in a rhythm as he bowls around the course, so that he can jump most of the fences out of that rhythm without having to slow down.

More bits, clockwise from top left: vulcanite pelham with curb chain and rubber guard; copper corkscrew with cheeks; copper double twisted wire with cheeks; cheek snaffle with soft twist; Dutch gag with rubber bit guards; Kimblewick; rubber gag. Centre: a brush is fitted to the side of the bit to help with steering.

Bridles and nosebands

In the interests of safety, the bridle and all other items of tack should be inspected on a regular basis to make sure that the stitching is still secure and that there are no areas of weakness that might cause the leather to snap. Particular attention should be paid to the folded areas, where the cheek pieces and reins are attached to the bit.

Needless to say, the bridle should also fit correctly. I have a preference for rubber reins, but some people would rather use web reins with leather grips. I have one objection to those; if you need to slip your reins, the grips can get in the way.

I normally use a flash noseband. This stops the horse from evading the bit by crossing its jaw or opening its mouth, but will not restrict the intake of air through its nostrils. Grackle figure-eight nosebands, which I sometimes use, have much the same effect.

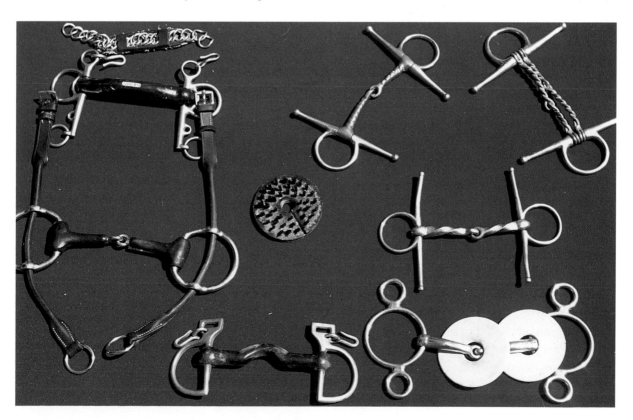

Above: *The Mark Todd jumping saddle.*

Right: *A selection of girths.*

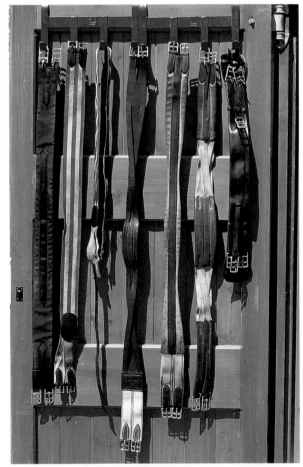

Saddles, girths and numnahs (saddle pads)

A jumping saddle is all that is needed for novice events, so long as it fits comfortably on the horse and sits the rider in the correct position. I normally use the same saddle (the close contact jumping one from my own range) for all three phases of novice competition. A dressage saddle is nice to have when you reach a higher level but, even then, it is not essential.

I used a jumping saddle for the dressage at an international three-day event in France, where I was riding Buddy Good who used to belong to Carolyn. He was a little horse and my legs would have been down around his knees if I had used a dressage saddle, so I chose one that allowed me to ride with my stirrups a bit shorter. Quite a few of the French riders do not use dressage saddles, so I was in good company.

For novice events, I use Cottage Craft (foam-padded cotton) girths which are cheap and practical. You can also use leather girths, which are excellent, but you must ensure that the stitching is checked on a regular basis. Whatever type you use, it is essential that the girths are in good condition. All my horses, whatever their level, wear an elasticated over-girth for the cross-country. Like the belt and braces theory, this is a safety-first measure which saves you from getting into trouble if something snaps.

We always use numnahs (saddle pads) under the saddle, normally the synthetic sheepskin type which is placed on top of a square pad made of quilted material. We have a variety of other smaller pads which can be used to make the saddle sit correctly on the horse's back.

Breast plates and martingales

Our horses always wear a breast plate for the show-jumping and cross-country phases. It helps to keep the saddle in place and I regard it as an essential piece of equipment. Martingales are only used if the horse is prone to throwing its head in the air, but they would never be tight. Horses can fight against the martingale, so I would not want mine to come into play until the horse's head was quite high. If using a martingale, you need to fit stoppers on the reins so that the rings cannot get caught up on the bit.

Rugs

The stabled horse will need clothing to keep him warm in winter. In most countries this normally means a stable rug, plus an underblanket for added warmth in cold weather. If kept at grass, he will need a waterproof New Zealand rug to protect him from rain as well as cold.

The requirements at an event will depend on the weather. If it is wet, some sort of waterproof protection such as a rain sheet is necessary. When it is wet it is often cold, so you would need a blanket under the waterproof covering — unless you were using a New Zealand rug, which is cumbersome but does combine the two requirements in one.

The one other necessary item of clothing is a Thermatex rug or a sweat sheet, which the horse will wear while he is cooling down after the cross-country, or drying off after he has been washed down. My own rugs come from the Horseware range, which are of good quality and very effective. There are plenty of other types of clothing, from travelling rugs to quarter sheets, on which you can spend your money, but you can get along perfectly well without them.

Leg protectors and bandages

Nowadays there are excellent boots on the market to protect the horse's front and hind legs on the cross-country phase. Traditionally they were made of leather with rubber lining, but the newer ones of synthetic material may give even better protection to the specific parts that need it. They have the added attraction of being fastened by velcro straps, which make them particularly easy to put on and take off.

I no longer use bandages when working the horse at home or riding him in a competition. It was once thought that they gave support to the legs, but I think that you can do more harm than good if you get the tension wrong. You can also do damage if the padding underneath the bandages gets creased. I just use open-fronted tendon protectors on the horse's forelegs for jumping. For schooling and hacking, the horses wear ordinary front boots; we only use back boots if they have a brushing problem behind.

All our horses wear over-reach boots for cross-country, though I believe there are both advantages and disadvantages with them. They obviously afford some protection if the horse does over-reach, but they can also cause a fall if he happens to tread on one. There have certainly been two instances when I've had falls for that reason. There may have been a third, because Just an Ace's inexplicable fall in the 1994 World Equestrian Games could have been caused by him treading on an over-reach boot. Whether or not this was the case, I shall never know. If the horse has a tendency to over-reach it definitely makes sense to protect his heels, but I would use

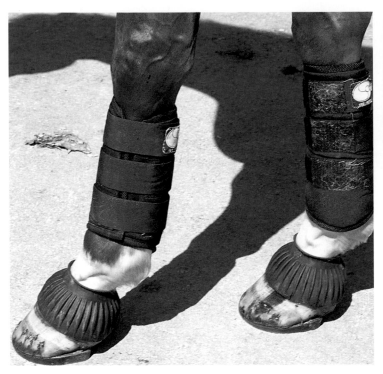

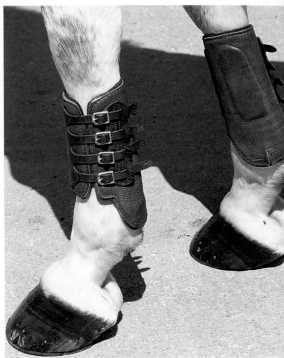

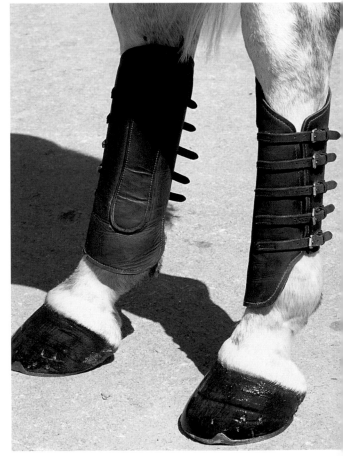

Above left: *Front cross-country boots with velcro fastening and over-reach boots.*

Above right: *Front cross-country boots made of leather.*

Right: *Hind cross-country boots.*

short boots which reduce the danger of him tripping up on them.

The only time our horses wear bandages on their legs is when they are travelling home after a competition, but they wouldn't automatically be put on the novices. I believe in keeping things as simple as possible and using common sense to decide on what is necessary. If the ground is good and the horse has finished without any nicks or cuts, we probably wouldn't bandage the novices.

But we do use bandages (with stable wraps underneath) when the ground is hard, which could mean throughout the summer months. In these circumstances, we would apply some form of leg cooling lotion under the bandages.

If the horse had knocked itself or hit a fence very hard, we would apply a poultice under a bandage which would remain on until the following morning. Both legs would be bandaged,

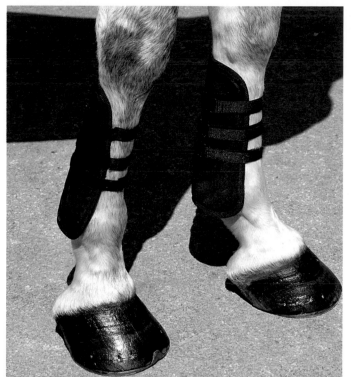

Above: *Two types of open-fronted tendon boots.*

Left:
Back fetlock boots.

even though the poultice is only applied to the damaged one.

We do not use bandages for extra warmth in the winter, partly because I like a horse to have as natural a lifestyle as possible. He would only wear them in the stable if he had filling in his legs or some other problem.

Studs and shoes

The only time I use studs on a novice horse is when the ground is very slippery, perhaps because of heavy rain after a long dry spell, or because a muddy surface had become very greasy. Under these conditions, it can be dangerous to go round the cross-country course without them.

Having said that, I am a great believer in getting the novice horse used to balancing himself if he does slip a little. It will teach him to be nimble on his feet. If he has support from studs on every

A selection of studs with hoof pick, spanner (wrench) and stud hole cleaner. A thread cleaner is in the centre.

occasion, he will never learn how to save himself. The concave shoes we use on all our horses, rather than flat road shoes, help to give a better foothold, though obviously not as much as one would get from studs.

Cross-country equipment for the rider

There are hard and fast rules concerning your own clothes and equipment as well as the horse's tack, so you need to read the rule book thoroughly. Some items are compulsory, while others are forbidden. If you do not comply with the rules, you face the threat of elimination, which would be a miserable way to bow out of your first one-day event.

I never use a stop-watch at one-day events, but I always wear spurs and carry a stick for the cross-country. These are useful, particularly on a green horse that's a bit spooky, as a back-up to the leg aid. However, spurs may not always be a good idea for the novice rider. They would be useful for getting a horse that tended to be a bit sticky

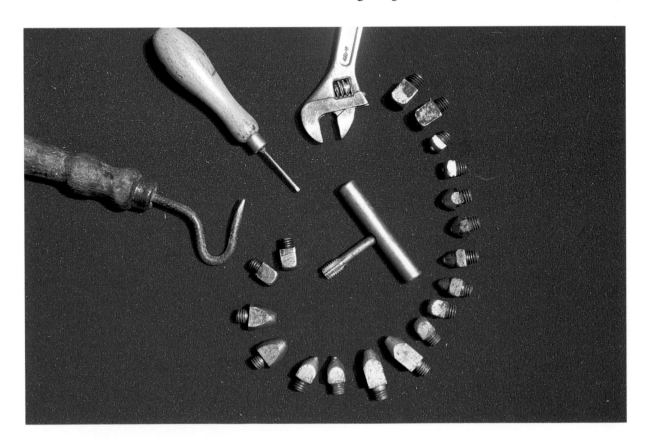

Ready to go across country. I am wearing a crash helmet with safety harness, a back protector, gloves and spurs. The horse is equipped with breast plate, cross-country boots and over-reach boots.

to go forward, but they would probably be a disadvantage if the horse were fairly hot-headed and difficult to hold.

An approved crash helmet, with correctly fitting harness, is compulsory for the cross-country at whatever level. In most countries, the same applies to a back protector, which you wear under or over your shirt or sweater. It is also a good idea to wear gloves and, unless it is stifling hot, something with long sleeves that will afford some protection against grazing or cuts. A stock or hunting tie is officially recommended for safety purposes, although I am far from convinced that it offers much protection. As a safety precaution, the tie pin should be removed before you ride across country.

Summary

Bitting
- Start with mild bit (e.g., loose-ring or eggbutt snaffle)
- If a horse is difficult to hold in show-jumping and cross-country, try a different bit for those phases
- Stronger snaffle bits include French link and Dr Bristol
- Avoid too strong a bit as the horse will not want to accept contact

General
- Check tack regularly for signs of weakness
- Check rule book for correct tack and clothing

Chapter 7

FINAL PREPARATIONS

You can learn more by competing than you ever can in a school, so I am a great believer in getting out and having a go, as long as you are reasonably well prepared. Obviously the horse and rider must be sufficiently confident to tackle a novice cross-country course. If this is your first event, it would be a good idea to start at the lowest level available.

I tend to treat the horse's first few events as a continuation of its training and would not have any thoughts of winning. Putting everything to the test is nevertheless helpful. Until you do so, you are never really sure which particular things need to be improved. Your first few events will give you a much clearer indication as to what you need to be working on at home.

Opposite: *Hunter trials will give the horse experience over natural fences.*

Dressage and show-jumping

I would want to make sure that the horse had been in something resembling a dressage arena, so that he gets used to working in a confined space. You can always mark out an arena at home, using jump poles, oil drums or something similar. Ideally it should be 20 x 40 m, which is the size used for the novice test. The arena can seem tiny if you have not worked the horse within these dimensions beforehand.

If he is used to working on an all-weather surface, it would be a good idea to mark out your arena in a field. He will be doing his test on grass, so he needs to get used to working on it. Competing in a few small dressage shows would be another useful part of his preparation.

You will need to learn the test thoroughly and maybe practise it a couple of times at home. It is not a good idea to ride the test more frequently,

Above: *Little dressage competitions help to prepare the horse for his first one-day event.*

Opposite: *Little show-jumping contests are also part of the preparation.*

because the horse then learns to anticipate and may start making transitions earlier than they are required. It is better to practise the movements in a different sequence. You should make sure that you know the test so well yourself that you don't have to think about it. That will leave you free to concentrate on what the horse is doing and getting him prepared for the next movement.

I would always advise the novice rider to do some little show-jumping contests before the horse competes in his first one-day event. Combined events, which also include dressage, would be another good idea. They would give horse and rider experience in two departments of eventing.

Cross-country

In addition to his cross-country schooling sessions, the horse could hunt or compete in hunter trials as part of his preparation. He needs to get used to tackling a wide variety of fences: water;

banks; ditches; combinations; angled fences; little corners, and so on. My aim is always to get the horse going into them with reasonable confidence, while maintaining his rhythm and without rushing. Once he can do that, I would be satisfied that he is sufficiently well prepared for his first one-day event.

Planning the day

It may be possible to inspect the cross-country fences the day before you jump them, which would allow you more time on the day of the competition. Otherwise you would probably need to allow an hour to walk the course and take in all you need to know about the route and obstacles. This can be done while the event is in progress, whereas the show-jumping course can only be walked before that phase begins, or during a break in the jumping, if there is one. This is something that you will need to find out in advance from the organiser.

Above: *A relaxing way to soak up the atmosphere.*

Left: *Make the most of any opportunity to ride the horse through water.*

Below left: *If possible, walk the cross-country course the day before the competition.*

You may also need to allow time to lunge the horse in order to get him settled before the dressage, which could take anything up to an hour. All these things need to be done quietly and calmly, which is only possible if you have allowed yourself ample time.

Turn-out

Horse and rider should obviously look their best. This means that the horse's mane will need to be pulled before the event and plaited (braided) on the day of the competition or, if more convenient because of an early start, the night before. The tail will need to be pulled or plaited (braided). Needless to say, your own clothes and the horse's tack will need to be clean and in good condition if you want to create a smart appearance.

Summary

For dressage and show-jumping
- Work the horse in a marked-out arena, preferably 20 x 40 m
- Compete in a few small dressage shows
- Learn the test thoroughly
- Compete in show-jumping contests (possibly combined with dressage)

For cross-country
- Get used to jumping a wide variety of fences
- Work at maintaining the horse's rhythm

Planning
- If possible, consider walking cross-country course the day before
- Allow yourself plenty of time on the day

Check-list for one horse competing in novice event — tack
bits
boots: exercise; show-jumping; and cross-country
breast plate
bridle (and spare)
dressage saddle and girth (optional)
elasticised over-girth
jumping saddle and girth
lunge equipment (if necessary)
martingale (if used) and rein stops
numnahs (saddle pads)
over-reach boots
spare girth and stirrup leathers
studs and stud kit — spanners (wrenchs), etc.

Rugs
rain sheet
roller and pad or surcingle
cooler or sweat sheet
wool/warm rug

Other items
baling twine
bandages and wraps
bridle rack (optional)
bucket(s)
feed and feed manger
fly repellent
grooming kit
hay and hay-net
hoof oil
hoof pick
insulating tape
leg coolant (to apply after cross-country when ground is hard)
plaiting (braiding) kit
saddle rack (optional)
scissors
scraper
spare head-collar (halter) and rope
spare tail bandage
sponges
towels
water

First Aid kit
animalintex poultice
antiseptic cream
cotton wool
disinfectant
elastic bandage
gamgee (gauze)
gauze pads
scissors
tape
wound powder

For the rider
back protector
copy of dressage test
correct clothes for three phases
gloves (and spare pair)
spare clothes (in case of falling in the water)
whip and spurs

Chapter 8

THE ONE-DAY HORSE TRIAL

The horse will have done some little dressage shows by the time he competes in his first one-day event, so the sight of horse-boxes and trailers and horses milling around will not be entirely new to him. If he were particularly highly strung or above himself, I would lunge him until he had settled down. Otherwise about half an hour's ridden work is probably enough for most horses before they do their test.

Preparation for the dressage test

At home my novice horses are rarely schooled for more than 20 minutes, so I would not want to do much more with them while preparing for the test. If the horse was quiet, I might only do

Above: *A good example of free walk on a long rein.*

Opposite: *The horse's front legs are slightly uneven, showing that he is still a bit green, but he is nevertheless making a good shape over this novice oxer.*

10–15 minutes. There is no point in grinding away if the horse doesn't need the work, he will only come to expect it or get tired and bored.

My preparation begins by walking and trotting the horse quietly around the warm-up area, letting him take in his surroundings. This would not, however, be done on a loose rein. I will be working him in a fairly long and low outline to begin with, and I expect him to accept contact as soon as I get on.

Young horses like to have a good look around and I allow them to do this within limits. If the horse is still looking away after two or three minutes, I tell him that it's now time to pay attention to me and concentrate. With a lazy type, I would obviously want to make sure that he was working forward. Otherwise I would try to keep him as relaxed as possible.

During the warm-up period I also practise transitions, circles and all the other movements that are included in the test. About five minutes

A nice outline for the canter.

The final halt is not quite square, but it was a good effort.

Saluting the judges.

before we were due to go into the arena, I would ask for a little more in the way of roundness and activity in the paces. Some riders jam the poor horse on the bit and keep hammering away for half an hour or so. As a result, the horse gets tired and thoroughly fed up to the point that he refuses to try any more.

Before you start your test, you need to discard your whip and the horse's leg protectors. Once, when helping Carolyn, I forgot to remove her horse's boots and she was promptly eliminated, which did not make me the hero of the hour! Riding into the arena with your whip is also penalised by elimination, so you need to know the rules thoroughly.

When you ride a youngster towards the arena, away from the place where he has been working with other horses, he can suddenly lose his confidence and concentration at finding himself on his own. When that happens, you have to make the best of it, putting your legs on to tell him to concentrate and using your hands to tell him to listen. You can then (hopefully) trot quietly around the arena while you wait for the signal to start.

Sometimes the horse needs to be told to concentrate and work properly in the arena.

Riding the dressage test

Remember that you are not trying to win at this stage, so there is nothing to get uptight about. Novice riders are inclined to freeze as soon as they get into the arena, and the horse then learns that it can do what it likes in there. If you think of the test as a schooling exercise, which provides another stage of progression in the horse's training, you are far more likely to keep riding positively. To a certain extent, I would still correct the horse in the arena so that he knows, right from the beginning, that when he is in there he is still expected to concentrate and listen to me.

Obviously you can't ignore the test, but you can avoid letting the horse think that he can get away with doing his own thing in the arena. For instance, if he wandered off the track or wasn't going forward enough, I would use my legs strongly to make him go forward. If he were running away from me, I would be prepared to do

an obvious half-halt in the arena to get him back.

A lot of riders throw away marks by being inaccurate. Nearly all the movements happen at a marker and you should be able to ride to the appropriate letter and make your transition (or start your new movement) at that precise point — not a couple of strides before or after. You can only be accurate when the horse is trained to make a transition exactly where and when you ask for it, which is why I practise this so frequently at home. You also have to train yourself to ride a circle, which is not supposed to be a shape with four more or less straight sides!

A couple of strides before each transition, I would do a very subtle half-halt which will tell the horse that something is about to happen. It might be no more than sitting up a little and squeezing with the hands and legs; if he is listening, this will be enough to prepare him for the next movement.

Back to good behaviour.

A good final halt.

I am not looking for much impulsion in a novice test, but I do want the horse to be active in all its paces. If he is working forward within an outline, he will have created a sufficient amount of energy (which is the meaning of impulsion) to perform the simple movements required.

By the end of the test you will probably have quite a good clue as to the areas on which you need to work. You can also find out from the judges' score sheet, which is a useful guide-line if you are fairly inexperienced and don't have a trainer present to tell you where you went wrong.

Walking the show-jumping course

Having ridden in some small jumping shows, you should be aware of anything that could make the horse a bit spooky. Maybe he is suspicious of any filling that is used in a fence; perhaps he is alarmed by the sight and sound of a flapping

tent. Or he might have a highly-developed homing instinct, which could mean that he is liable to duck out at any fence close to the exit of the arena because he is thinking of getting back to his horse-box or trailer. You need to be aware of such possibilities so that you know which fences you will have to ride more positively.

The start flags are the first things to look for when you walk the show-jumping course. It is easy to overlook them in your anxiety to inspect the fences, but you need to make sure that you go through them if you want to avoid elimination. You will obviously need to learn your way around, while working out the best route to jump each fence. You don't want to cut corners too sharply or go unnecessarily wide.

You should also make a mental note of anything that might cause the horse to spook or take away his concentration. If there are any such

The horse is given a pat as he leaves the arena on a long rein.

places, you will need to ride a bit more strongly when you come to them. When you pass the last fence, you also need to look for the finish. I speak from experience, having done most things wrong in the course of my eventing career. These include missing out a show-jump on one occasion and failing to go through the finish on another.

The first couple of fences will normally be straightforward, but you still need to consider how you will approach them. You will also be looking for the different turns you will have to make and, if this involves a change of rein, whether the horse will do a flying change or will have to be brought back to trot. You will know from practising at home — and from your little jumping shows — whether the horse normally changes legs at canter when you change direction. Some horses do this naturally, while others

become disunited and have to come back to trot before you ask them to canter again on the correct lead.

Related fences

You should have taught yourself to walk the distance between related fences by taking steps that are 90 cm (3 ft) long. It is easy enough to set out measurements at home so that you get your striding right and can measure up to 18 m (60 ft) with reasonable accuracy. The average length of a horse's stride is 3.6 m (12 ft), so four of your steps should equal one of his. You also have to allow for landing and take-off.

If you were measuring the distance between two elements of a double, you would walk two steps (1.8 m/6 ft) to reach the approximate place where the horse will land. Another four steps (3.6 m/12 ft) will tell you where he will be after he has taken one stride. Assuming this is a one-stride double, two more steps will take you to the second element. In other words, the normal distances between the two parts of a double would be 7.3 m (24 ft) if the horse is to take one non-jumping stride and 11 m (36 ft) if he is to take two. Obviously it is important for the rider to know which it will be.

In novice eventing, I would regard any two fences that allowed for five strides or less between them to be on a related distance. That may sound a lot, but in pure show-jumping you would be looking at eight or nine stride distances as related. Most novice event courses are built using the correct distances, but you should not rely on it. You might come across one that is, for example, 90 cm (3 ft) short of a normal four-stride distance. You would therefore make a mental note to ride a little steadier at the first of these related fences in order to avoid getting too close to the second one.

Watching other competitors

It would be a good idea to spend a little time watching the show-jumping on your feet rather than on the horse, preferably when there are good riders in the ring. This will confirm the distances between related fences and tell you whether any of them need to be ridden in a forward way or, perhaps, whether they require the horse to steady back.

At the same time, you have to bear in mind that horses have different lengths of stride. If you are watching one with a huge great stride, you would hardly want to adopt the same methods if you are about to ride a little, short-striding horse.

Getting ready for the show-jumping

My novice horses just wear open-fronted tendon boots for protection in the show-jumping phase. You can also use over-reach boots and back fetlock boots, which are a good idea if the horse has a tendency to knock into himself.

As already mentioned, I only use studs if the ground is slippery. Unless the horse had just done his dressage and was already warmed up, I would like to get on him about 20 minutes before he show-jumps and would start jumping when there are five or six horses to go before mine.

Ideally, I would start my jumping practice by trotting over a little cross-pole a couple of times. Then I would jump an upright four or five times, starting very low and building up. After that I would do exactly the same with an oxer. It doesn't always work out this way when you have a lot of horses to ride. Sometimes I only have time for a couple of practice jumps before I go into the arena. But you would certainly want to avoid that if you were a beginner. With careful planning (and only one horse to ride), it is possible to give yourself plenty of time if you plan your day carefully.

You need to have someone to help you with the practice fences, otherwise you have to put up with the heights that other people are jumping. Having said that, you are normally lucky to get one fence to yourself in England, so you can't always get what you want — even with a willing helper.

Some people jump 30 or more fences before they even go into the ring which, to my mind, is crazy. If the horse was going badly, you would obviously want to jump a few more fences to get him going properly, but there is no point in jumping just for the sake of it. The horse needs to reserve his energy for the fences in the ring, not the practice ones outside.

When you have finished with the practice jumps, you should have time to ride around quietly and go through the course in your head to make sure that you remember it. If the horse is liable to get upset, I would just walk around on a fairly loose rein and let him relax. If he were on the lazy side, I would give him a short, sharp canter to have him awake and ready for his round. When you finally go into the ring, don't forget to wait for the starting signal (it could be a bell, whistle or hooter) before you start.

Riding the show-jumping course

Novice riders often find it difficult to stay relaxed. As with the dressage, they tend to freeze as soon as they get into the arena. The show-jumping phase should not be regarded as a big deal. Like the dressage, it should be seen as a training competition — at least for the first few events. If you start worrying about the fences, you will only make the horse more tense.

A common mistake is to ride each fence as though it were a single obstacle and not part of a course. Your main aim should be to establish a rhythm and get the horse jumping in that rhythm, without allowing him to rush. You are riding a course not a succession of single fences, and you want to make it flow. That means keeping the horse balanced and moving along in a forward canter, jumping fences as they come.

Normally the fences at novice level can be jumped in the same rhythm. The correct speed (based on a 3.6 m/12 ft canter stride) is more forward than a working canter. If you can maintain it, you should be exactly right for any related fences — assuming that the course builder has used the correct distances, which would normally be the case at novice level. If the horse loses his rhythm and goes a bit too fast or slows down, you will have to do something about it, either by steadying him or asking him to go forward.

Above: *Early warm-up for the show-jumping. Carolyn is using a placing pole in front of the cross-poles.*

Below: *Jumping an upright in the practice area, with a take-off rail in front of the fence.*

Jumping two fences on a related distance. As the horse lands, he spooks and backs off the second fence, so the rider reacts quickly and uses a strong driving seat (picture 3) which enables him to make the distance to the second fence and get a good jump over it.

Or there might be times when he jumps a fence and runs on, in which case you may be able to use a turn to the next fence to get him to steady back and regain his rhythm and balance. If the horse happens to become disunited after turning, there is no need to get in a fluster about it. Keep calm and take your time to bring him back to trot, then ask for the correct lead and carry on.

If I felt that the horse was trying to spook or to back off the fence, I would sit down, using my seat and legs strongly (and, if necessary, the whip) to get him over the obstacle. I would not worry too much about rolling a pole off it; the more important thing is that the horse learns that he must get from one side to the other when presented to a fence.

Walking the cross-country course

If you are new to the sport and you have an opportunity to walk the course the day before the event, it makes sense to do so. Until you get used to the idea of walking courses, it can be quite difficult to memorise the whole thing. You may even want to walk the course twice to get it clearly fixed in your mind.

Needless to say, you should avoid going round with a bunch of friends and chatting the whole way. If you do this you are likely to get to the end and realise that you can scarcely remember any of the fences. You will need to have a clear picture of the course in your mind, because you will not be able to ride in a positive way unless you know where to go and what to jump next.

By now you should have practised over every type of cross-country fence, but if you do happen to find something that is unfamiliar there is no need to panic. You have to trust the horse to a certain extent, and you have to ride him in a way that makes him confident in his own ability to jump anything he meets.

Walking the cross-country course follows much the same principle as inspecting the show-jumps. You have to learn the route and decide on the best line and speed for your approach to each fence. You also need to walk the distances in any combination to determine the number of strides and you must be aware of anything that might worry or distract the horse. With a youngster, you have to work on the assumption that he might look suspiciously at anything, which means that you have to be prepared to ride in a very positive way.

You will also be looking at the situation of each fence, whether it is on the flat, uphill, downhill, out on its own or close to another obstacle. Perhaps there is one going from sunlight into a dark wood, or one where the sunlight may be likely to shine straight in your eyes. If I thought that the horse might spook at one or more particular fence, I would decide to steady the pace and become really positive in my approach. I might even plan to come back to trot. You need to reduce the speed well in advance, so that the horse is going at the right pace half a dozen strides away from the fence.

There could be some downhill steps or, perhaps, a little palisade with a drop where I might decide that the horse would get a better view of the obstacle if he were to take it from trot. This would also give me time to counter any possible hesitation by having him strongly between leg and hand, keeping him straight and going forward.

As mentioned in the training chapter, it is counter-productive to go flat out into a fence if you think the horse might stop at it. Speed can actually make it easier for him to duck out. On the other hand he may launch himself over, but he would probably frighten himself in the process and so set his training right back.

You will need to sit up at certain types of fences, decreasing the pace to ride them like show-jumps, and again making your adjustments so that you are at the right pace half a dozen strides away. Such obstacles include combinations, downhill fences, drops, bank-type obstacles and coffins. The horse needs to be balanced and going steadily into these fences, but always staying in front of your leg so that he doesn't lose the desire to go forward. At most other obstacles, whether uprights or spreads, you will be able to let the horse bowl along and take the fences out of his stride.

Getting ready for the cross-country

The horse will need to have protective boots on all four legs before going across country. Mine would also have over-reach boots on his forelegs, plus an over-girth, breast plate and, possibly, a martingale. I do not use grease on the horse's legs at one-day events and I only use studs when the ground is slippery. If time permits, my horse's mane will be unplaited (unbraided) between the show-jumping and the cross-country, because there might be the odd occasion when I want to hang onto it.

I will be wearing a back protector, gloves and spurs — and I will be carrying a stick. I never use a stop-watch at one-day events. To my mind, riders should learn to use their own judgement as to the speed at which they're going instead of relying on a stop-watch the whole time. In any case, it would be extremely difficult to work out where you should be at a given time on a one-day event course.

If the horse had just done his show-jumping, he would already be warmed up for the cross-country. I would nevertheless jump the practice fence a few times just to let him know which phase is coming next. If he had been standing in the horse-box or trailer for a while, I would allow time for him to have a walk, trot and canter before having a few jumps over the practice fence. Immediately before the cross-country start, I would walk the horse round on a loose rein if he needed to relax, but with more sense of purpose if he was on the lazy side. This is no time to let him slop around and go to sleep; he has to be fully awake, knowing that soon he has another job to do.

Riding the cross-country course

Most people come into eventing because they are excited by the idea of riding a cross-country

Relaxing before the start of the cross-country.

course. If they wanted to do dressage or show-jumping, they could do them separately, or sometimes both together, so the cross-country must be the main attraction.

Most riders are likely to feel some anxiety mixed with excitement before they start, but they usually feel much happier when they are on their way — and happier still when they have finished! That bit of anxiety is quite normal, but if anyone were to feel so scared as to be unable to ride properly it could mean that he or she has chosen the wrong sport. After all, it is something that we are supposed to be doing for pleasure.

When the horse comes out of the start-box, I like to get him going at once. That does not mean setting off at a wild gallop; I simply want to give him a sense of purpose and direction. Those that are new to the sport can get a bit lost and start drifting around at the start and between fences. The rider might have seen it all before, but the horse is likely to find the whole scene very strange.

If the horse is hesitant and inclined to drift, it is up to the rider to say: 'Come on, we're going forward — there's the next fence so let's get to it'. That may call for a firm hold on the reins and a good kick or a slap with the stick. You don't want him going forward in a crazy, flat-out fashion, but you do want his attention to be focused on what he has to do. I would certainly want to be quicker than show-jumping pace, except at those fences which necessitate jumping at that speed, but it would be more of a purposeful forward canter than a disorderly gallop.

Time should not be of prime importance at the horse's first few events. The same applies if you are a novice rider, even if you are competing on an experienced horse. Initially you should concentrate on getting the horse going in a nice rhythm and jumping cross-country fences correctly, rather than racing round trying to get close to the optimum time. Increasing the pace will come later, when you and the horse have

In the start-box, ready to set off with a sense of purpose.

Opposite: *I have my seat and lower leg in the driving position coming to the edge of this drop. The horse has a good look and then jumps off boldly.*

The galloping position.

learnt to jump the fences in balance and rhythm.

If you feel the need to slow down for each obstacle, you are probably going too fast. On the other hand, if the horse is being a bit hesitant you may be going too slowly. In this case a strong leg aid or a slap with the stick will remind him that he must keep going forward.

Some riders kick like fury when they are coming into a fence, even when the horse is already going quite fast and jumping boldly. As a result, he goes galloping away from the obstacle and the rider has to grab him back and fight for control.

It would be much more effective to tone the whole thing down and start to trust the horse to jump the fences, without feeling that it is necessary to boot him into every one of them.

You will obviously have set out with the intention of completing the course, but if the horse isn't happy and you've had a series of refusals, you would be wise to pull up and retire. If you carried on, you would run the risk of getting the horse into serious trouble. It would be better to take time off for more schooling before you compete again.

The horse jumps up these two little steps very boldly.

I have to sit back and keep contact to help him fit in the short stride to the upright.

1

2

A more experienced novice jumping boldly into water. I have slipped my reins a little, but maintained contact and kept the horse cantering through the water.

After the finish

The horse needs to remain in balance after he has gone through the finish, so that he can be pulled up smoothly. Injuries can easily occur if you come to an abrupt halt, or if you express your delight by dropping the reins and throwing your arms around the horse's neck. He will then start using his forelegs as brakes, putting unnecessary stress on them. By all means give him a hug after

Opposite: Jumping a double of corners on one of the more difficult novice courses. Note that the horse and rider's eyes are firmly fixed on the next element.

you have pulled up and dismounted, but not before.

Completing the course means different things to different people — some are just happy that they are still alive! I have seen inexperienced riders come back elated after completing a novice course, even when they've had a stop along the way. At my stage, I can still get a real buzz out of a young horse jumping really well across country at his first few novice events. When that happens, you can start hoping that you have a future star.

Summary

Preparation for the dressage test
- Lunge horse if he is highly strung or above himself; otherwise half an hour's ridden work should be enough
- Allow horse to take in his surroundings
- Practise transitions and other movements from the test
- Do not go into the arena carrying your whip
- Remove horse's boots before the test

Riding the dressage test
- Treat first few events as part of horse's schooling
- Start each new movement at appropriate marker
- Try to keep the horse active in each pace

Walking the show-jumping course
- Make sure that you know position of start and finish flags
- Work out your best route
- Look out for anything that might cause horse to spook
- Walk distances between combinations and related fences

Riding the show-jumping course
- Stay as relaxed as possible
- Establish a rhythm and let the horse jump out of same tempo
- Try to make the course flow
- Ride positively

Walking the cross-country course
- Decide on the best way to approach each fence
- Walk the distances in combinations and related fences
- Be aware of anything that might distract the horse
- Decide which fences will need a slower approach
- Make sure that you have a mental picture of the course

Riding the cross-country course
- Set off with a sense of purpose
- Do not go at a mad gallop
- Aim to get horse in rhythm and balance
- Concentrate on jumping fences correctly
- Do not worry about optimum time at first few events
- Keep horse in balance coming through the finish

Chapter 9

MAKING PROGRESS

When I am starting a young horse in eventing, I like to do three or four novice classes in quick succession, possibly within ten days or two weeks. Those of us who are based in England have a big enough programme of events to be able to do that, but it may not be possible in other countries. If you can do them in a block, it will help the rider as well as the horse. Both will be learning through the competitions. When there is a gap of two weeks between events, the horse tends to forget what he learnt the last time which means that you go back to square one.

Obviously I need to be sure that the horse is physically capable of this sort of schedule and that it will not be detrimental to its well-being. If he were only a five-year-old, I would need to be extremely careful not to overdo the number of competitions. I also need to be aware of the terrain; it would be asking for trouble if I were to run him in quick succession on very heavy-going ground or deep mud. Whatever plans you are making, the horse's welfare has to come first.

Having said that, you will not be running him fast across country at his first few events, so you will not be taking a lot out of him. He will just be going there to further his education.

After those initial three or four competitions, I would give the horse a couple of weeks' break from eventing before doing another block. During the break he can do flat work and jumping at home, paying particular attention to the shortcomings that were revealed during the competitions. He could also do some little jumping and dressage shows. Normally there is a definite improvement when the horse comes back to his next block of events. After the second batch is completed, I might turn him out to rest for a few weeks.

Gaining experience

Sometimes a horse can be very calm in the dressage at his first event and get fairly het up at his next appearance. This is because he has learnt what to expect and knows there is the excitement of the cross-country to come. It may take another couple of events before he settles again. He has to learn that there is a definite pattern, and that the cross-country (at least in most countries) comes much later.

Young horses often go through patches when they seem to get better. At other times they seem to regress for an event or two, before improving again. It is unhelpful to try and judge his progress from one event to the next. You are better off taking a long-term view and judging it over a period of three or four months. If there is no progress during that time, you will know that you are on the wrong track and in need of help.

It may be that your horse has done half a dozen events and is still being spooky, or is difficult in some other way. If you are a novice rider, you should get the opinion of someone experienced who could possibly try to sort out the problem by riding the horse in the school or at a competition. Otherwise, if you encounter problems at every event, the horse is learning nothing and therefore going nowhere, and you need to do something about it.

If the rider is a novice, the chances are that the horse's problems stem from the way he is being ridden. On the other hand, it could mean that he is not cut out for eventing or that he is unsuitable for the rider. Not all horses are natural eventers. Sometimes no amount of training will make them into good performers across country, in which case perseverance may actually be detrimental to both horse and rider. The opinion of someone experienced could help you to decide whether it would be better to look for a more suitable horse.

After one of my horses has done five or six events, I would hope that I could look back and realise that he had become more used to working in an arena of 20 x 40 m and that he had become more attentive to me. I would also like to find that he was standing straighter in his halts, was keeping a better rhythm in all his paces, and that his transitions were smoother and more balanced.

You can't expect all these things to happen quickly, but it can often be encouraging to think back on how the horse was going a few months earlier and, whatever his recent regressions, realise that he has made some definite improvement during the intervening time.

Stepping up the pace

Once the horse is jumping confidently around novice cross-country courses, you can begin to think about getting closer to the optimum time. I like my pupils to use their own judgement in this respect. If they have 20 or so penalties when they first attempt to get close to the optimum, they will know that they need to be a bit faster next time out. In this way they eventually learn, while still at novice level, the speed required to keep time penalties to a minimum.

If you find it difficult to judge the speed, it could be helpful to go cantering with someone more experienced who knows what is needed. The first time, you could canter together at a fairly steady cross-country pace and then increase the speed a bit on the next time out. This would give you an idea of the pace required, which you cannot be expected to know if you have never been eventing before.

I would not consider going fast across country unless I had a chance of getting a place. If you've had a bad dressage and a couple of fences down in the show-jumping, it seems crazy to go like 'a bat out of hell' on the cross-country. It simply serves to wind the horse up and to run him into the ground for no purpose. If I had a reasonable dressage and a clear round in the show-jumping, I would certainly think about having a go at getting into the placings. This is the time for working towards being more competitive in the novice grades.

Opposite: Carolyn has moved up to intermediate classes. She has slipped her reins a little in preparation for the drop landing, at the same time keeping contact but in no way interfering with the horse. She is sitting up, with her lower leg in a good, strong position.

New movements

All our horses start learning new movements well before they move out of novice events. They will have to perform new things when they move up to the next level, so I like them to be included at an early stage so that I have time to work on improving them.

Transitions

The horse will have to get used to transitions that are more demanding. Instead of the simple halt to walk and walk to trot, I will be asking him to go straight from halt to trot and from walk to canter. He will also have to learn more demanding downward transitions, such as canter/walk. Assuming that the simple transitions have been properly established, this should not cause much of a problem. On the other hand, you should not expect instant perfection.

The horse has to learn what you mean by the slightly stronger aids that tell him, for instance, that you want to move from halt to trot. If he does not move forward into trot, you will need to strengthen the leg aids a little more. If that still

Moving up a gear. Though we are going faster, my position has scarcely altered. I am straight back into the galloping position after landing.

doesn't work, the aids will have to be backed up by the stick or spur so that the horse understands what you are asking him to do. He is not supposed to dribble into trot, having walked half a dozen steps before going into the pace you want. He cannot be expected to get the message instantly, but he should be training towards the correct transition.

Simple change

The simple change in canter is another test of the horse's ability to perform smooth and accurate transitions. He will be required to come back from canter, initially through trot, and to take a few steps in walk before striking off into canter on the other leg. He will have learnt how to do these separately, so it is simply a matter of putting them together and working to make that happen in a flowing way.

Medium paces

Medium trot and canter (as performed in the lengthened strides that the horse has already learnt) will need to be improved. They require the horse to lengthen his stride, keeping the same rhythm while going into a slightly longer outline. This can be difficult to achieve, especially if the horse is naturally short-striding. The tendency is for him to run faster, which means that the rhythm is changed. A common mistake is for riders to let go of the horse's front end and then start kicking, with the invariable result that the horse goes hollow and begins to run faster.

You cannot expect to achieve medium paces instantly, unless the horse is exceptionally talented in that direction. Initially he would be asked to lengthen for half a dozen strides of trot, or canter, possibly on a circle. To do this you need to keep contact with the hands and ask with the seat and legs for the horse to take longer steps. If he ends up running faster, you will need to tell him that this is not what you want. This is done by bringing him back to a balanced working trot and then asking again.

The horse should stay light on the forehand, otherwise it will be difficult for him to use his shoulders properly and give the extra push from the hocks. If he does tend to run onto his forehand, particularly in canter, I would only ask for three or four lengthened strides so that he doesn't have time to get lower on the shoulder and heavy in front. Then I would get him back, balance him and ask again. In the beginning you will sometimes have to ask him to go quite a bit faster until he gets an idea of what is required of him.

Counter-canter

For an intermediate test, the horse has to learn to canter on a 5 m (16 ft) loop — away from the long side of the arena and back to it — without changing his leading leg. This is his introduction to counter-canter, of which a more difficult version will be required at advanced level. I would begin teaching the exercise by steering the horse off the track for just 2–3 m (6–9 ft) before moving back to it on a fairly gentle curve.

You would begin by cantering around the arena, for example, on the right rein, which means that the horse should be between your right leg and left hand. Then you need to steer

him 2–3 m (6–9 ft) away from the long side of the arena, while maintaining the aids for right canter. That is to say: right leg just behind the girth, left leg further back, with the right hand keeping a little flexion to the right.

When the horse is 2–3 m (6–9 ft) off the track, you should use your left hand to guide him back to it. It is only at this particular point that the horse will be asked to go on a left-handed curve (while leading on his right leg) for a few strides of correct counter-canter. He should then return to the track on a straight line.

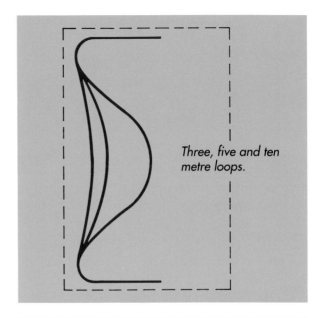

Three, five and ten metre loops.

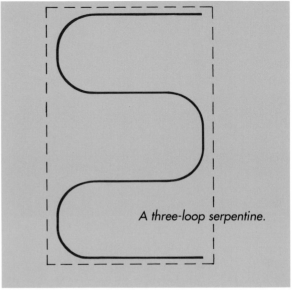

A three-loop serpentine.

A common mistake is for the rider to have the horse's neck bent far too much to the right and, instead of guiding him back to the track with the hand, pushing him back with the leg so that he is moving sideways. The horse finds this difficult and he will probably end up changing legs. You need to concentrate on keeping the horse's shoulders in front of you during this exercise; they should neither drop to the left nor swing to the right. If he changes legs, which usually happens because he has dropped his left shoulder, you need to correct him and try again.

Once the horse has learnt to do these little loops in a nice, smooth way, you can gradually increase the size to 4.5 m (15 ft) and then 9 m (30 ft). Later, perhaps, you could go right across the school in a serpentine, so that the counter-canter becomes more definite. In counter-canter to the left, the horse would be moving on a left-handed loop while leading on his right leg, with his body slightly bent towards the leading leg.

Rein-back

When I am teaching rein-back, I like to have the horse facing towards a wall or fence, so that he cannot move forward. I would want him to be rounded into the hand at halt, because he cannot rein-back correctly if he is hollow. I then lighten my weight on the horse's back by leaning slightly forward. At the same time I resist with the hands and use pressure from the lower legs (which are moved back slightly) to tell him that I want him to move. Because there is something solid in front of him, the one obvious way to go is backwards. Initially I might get just one step back, then I would immediately relax and pat the horse

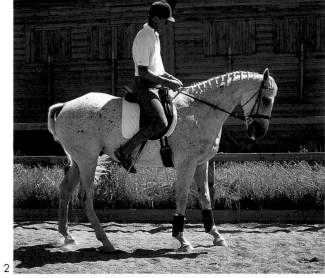

1

2

3

Right: Rein-back. I am exaggerating the aid with the lower leg, making it very clear to the horse that I want him to step back. He is rounded between my leg and hand at halt. I am resisting with the hand — but not pulling back — and the horse takes a step back. Initially he is showing some resistance, but then he relaxes. I am not sitting heavily in the saddle and the position of my hands stays the same throughout the movement.

before taking one step forward again. The next time I might ask for two steps back.

Some horses catch on very quickly; others seem incapable of grasping what it is that you are asking them to do. It is often helpful to have someone on the ground, who can put a hand just above the horse's chest and give him a push in the right direction while speaking the instruction: 'Back'. At the same time the rider will be giving the correct aids through hand, leg and weight of the body.

The last thing that you should do is plant yourself in the middle of a field, lean back and haul on the reins, expecting the horse to go back.

That would result in him raising his head, hollowing his back and, in all probability, refusing to budge. The chances are that the rider then gets angry and starts kicking and pulling until the horse is thoroughly upset. You then have a serious problem, because he will get tense whenever you come to a halt and you will not only have trouble with the rein-back; it will also be difficult to get him to stand still at the halt.

Jumping

I would hope that the show-jumping training at home and the competitions will have improved the way the horse approaches his fences and

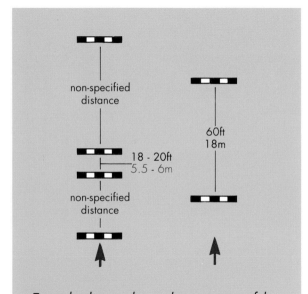

Trot poles that can be used at any stage of the horse's training. The 5.5–6 m (18–20 ft) distance represents one canter stride, but you could make one or two transitions within this line.

For example, you could trot over the first, walk over the second and trot on for the remaining two. The poles on the right could be used to practise changing the number of canter strides, starting with six. You could then try to get anything between five and nine strides by altering the speed and rhythm of the canter. This is a good exercise for teaching the horse to shorten and lengthen his canter stride.

A canter circle of three small fences.

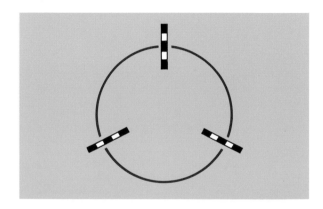

Practising related distances over two fences of 90 cm (3 ft) or more in height. The 18 m (60 ft) distance represents four strides and 22 m (72 ft) will be five strides. It is important to maintain the rhythm throughout, keeping each stride the same length.

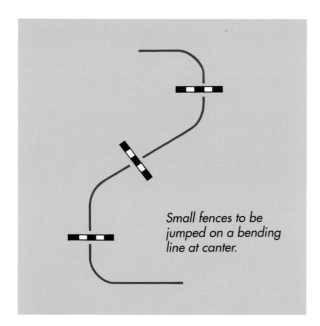

Small fences to be jumped on a bending line at canter.

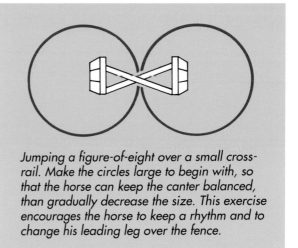

Jumping a figure-of-eight over a small cross-rail. Make the circles large to begin with, so that the horse can keep the canter balanced, than gradually decrease the size. This exercise encourages the horse to keep a rhythm and to change his leading leg over the fence.

Below: Jumping a one-stride double on an intermediate course. The horse lowers himself in preparation for take-off.

1

Jumping a one-stride double on an intermediate course. Horse and rider remain balanced in the middle of the

3

combination and jump the second part well. I have the correct lower leg position throughout.

comes away from them. Once he has started competing, I do very little jumping in the school unless I have a problem to sort out. Otherwise, I would do occasional gymnastic exercises to make sure that the horse is maintaining the correct shape. I might also introduce more difficult lines of fences, which could include related distances.

As the flat work and balance improves, it will be possible to make tighter turns into the obstacles and do more shortening and lengthening between the fences. You can use the distances in grids to teach the horse to adjust its length of stride. Apart from helping to educate the horse, these exercises would help to sharpen a novice rider's eye.

Summary

After about six events the horse should be:
- More attentive to the rider
- Maintaining a better rhythm in his paces
- Making smoother and more balanced transitions
- Jumping with greater accuracy and confidence
- Getting closer to the optimum cross-country time

Aids
- Medium trot and canter
- Start by asking the horse to lengthen for six strides
- Keep contact with hands
- Using seat and legs, ask for longer strides
- If horse runs faster, bring him back and ask again

Counter-canter
- Start with 2–3 m (6–9 ft) loops
- Maintain aids for canter according to horse's leading leg

For canter with right leg leading:
- Right leg just behind girth
- Left leg further back
- Right hand asks for a little flexion to the right

Rein-back
- Start by facing the horse towards a wall or fence
- Lean slightly forward to lighten weight
- Apply pressure with lower legs
- Resist with hands

A canter grid, using poles within the single canter stride between each oxer. These encourage the horse to look where he is going, and to use his neck and back so that he becomes rounder over the fences. Start with just two oxers and then add to them.

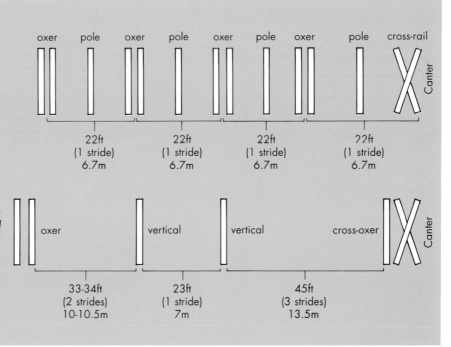

oxer	pole	oxer	pole	oxer	pole	oxer	pole	cross-rail

22ft (1 stride) 6.7m	22ft (1 stride) 6.7m	22ft (1 stride) 6.7m	22ft (1 stride) 6.7m

Canter

Another canter grid. If the horse's training is correct, he should complete this line of fences at the same speed that he approached them. You will need to go back to the exercises over poles if he starts rushing; they will help to make him wait and listen.

oxer	vertical	vertical	cross-oxer

33-34ft (2 strides) 10-10.5m	23ft (1 stride) 7m	45ft (3 strides) 13.5m

Canter

LOOKING TO THE FUTURE

You may now be thinking beyond the confines of this book and have your sights set on upgrading to a higher level. Our horses normally stay in novice classes until they have won their way up each rung of the ladder, by which time they should be ready to move into the next grade.

You don't necessarily have to wait for that to happen before you tackle your first three-day event; if the horse is jumping confidently across country, there is no reason why you should not attempt a novice three-day event. If so, you will need to get help in preparing a more rigorous fitness programme for the horse and yourself. The steeplechase section and the roads and tracks make the three-day test far more demanding on stamina, so the preparation has to be more regimented.

You may have ambitions to go right to the top. It will take at least two years (and probably more) before you and the horse are ready for a three-day event at three- or four-star level, but that distant goal can be the great incentive to keep you on the path of progress. I hope that I have helped to start you off on the right track and that you enjoy the continuing fascination of training your horse for this great all-round challenge.

INDEX